COMMUNICATING
EFFECTIVELY
IN ENGLISH

SECOND EDITION

COMMUNICATING
EFFECTIVELY
IN ENGLISH

Oral Communication for Non-Native Speakers

PATRICIA A. PORTER and
MARGARET GRANT
San Francisco State University

WADSWORTH PUBLISHING COMPANY

Belmont, California
A Division of Wadsworth, Inc.

English Editor: Angela Gantner
Editorial Assistant: Tricia Schumacher
Production Editor: Deborah Cogan
Managing Designer: Carolyn Deacy
Print Buyer: Barbara Britton
Permissions Editor: Peggy Meehan
Designer: Adriane Bosworth
Copy Editor: Thomas Briggs
Photographer: Pamela Gentile
Cartoonist: Stephen Kongsle
Compositor: G & S Typesetters, Inc.
Cover Illustration: Mark Stearney
Printer: Malloy Lithographing, Inc.

This book is printed on acid-free paper that meets Environmental Protection Agency standards for recycled paper.

1 2 3 4 5 6 7 8 9 10—95 94 93 92 91

Library of Congress Cataloging-in-Publication Data

Porter, Patricia A., 1939–
    Communicating effectively in English: oral communication for non-native speakers / Patricia A. Porter and Margaret Grant.—2nd ed.
      p. cm.
    Includes index.
    ISBN 0-534-17268-7
    1. English language—Textbooks for foreign speakers. 2. Oral communication. I. Grant, Margaret, 1935– . II. Title.
PE1128.P5924 1992
428.3'4—dc20   91-34679

Contents

Unit 2

**GETTING INFORMATION: INTERVIEWS
AND CONFERENCES   29**

Unit 3

PROVIDING INFORMATION: INSTRUCTIONS AND DEMONSTRATIONS   61

Unit 5

PERSUADING OTHERS: SOLVING A PROBLEM   151

Unit 6

Appendix

Preface

This book has been designed to help non-native speakers of English gain proficiency in speaking and listening. It is intended for use in college classes, intensive English programs, and English training courses for professionals. The materials are designed for a semester-long course but can be adapted for other time frames.

We believe that students can best learn communication skills by extensive practice. The book thus takes an *interactive, experiential approach* to learning. This means that the major emphasis is on activities that promote learner involvement and interaction, with students practicing the skills that are to be learned rather than just talking or hearing about them.

We also believe that students need to build their oral communication skills over a period of time: not everything about delivery, content, appropriate language, and good listening can be learned at once. Thus, we have designed the book for *cumulative learning,* moving from simpler tasks to more complex ones, focusing on different features of the speaking/listening process throughout, and working toward a final integration of a variety of skills.

The contents of the second edition have been reorganized in line with our experience teaching the text as well as with suggestions made by other teachers and reviewers, and they have been extensively classroom tested. The major activities of each unit are now as follows:

- *Unit 1. Understanding Your Audience and Being Understood*
  Surveying class members to learn about classmates' interests and presenting results of the survey to the class.

- *Unit 2. Getting Information: Interviews and Conferences*
  Interviewing a classmate and having a conference with someone outside of class (for example, a boss or a professor) and reporting on your interview and conference.

xv

- *Unit 3. Providing Information: Instructions and Demonstrations*
  Giving a presentation to demonstrate a process or provide instructions.

- *Unit 4. Providing Information: Group Discussions and Presentations*
  Holding a small-group discussion to share information on a topic, then presenting an informative group report to the class.

- *Unit 5. Proposing Changes: Solving a Problem*
  Giving an oral presentation to describe a problem and argue for a specific solution.

- *Unit 6. Persuading Others: Taking a Position*
  Giving an oral presentation individually and/or as a panel to argue in favor of a position on a controversial issue.

The actual number of units in the book has been reduced, but the second edition preserves the same general pattern of progression from informative speeches to persuasive speeches. The revised organization reflects the increasing difficulty of the cognitive demands of the six major assignments. In the first three units, students work with information that is known to them or learned through interviews. In the last three units, students must work with information from more challenging outside sources, such as articles and reference materials in the library. The first four units focus on informative presentations, while the last two include expanded guidelines and practice in argumentation.

As in the first edition, speech assignments allow for individual and group presentations: pair or small-group presentations are featured in Units 1 and 4, while individual presentations are the focus in Units 2, 3, and 5. Unit 6 is structured for individual speeches and/or panel presentations. (The impromptu opinion speech assignment that served as the focus of a unit in the previous edition has been incorporated as an activity in Unit 6.)

In keeping with our belief in the necessity of extensive practice for success in oral communication, we have expanded the number of practice activities in the second edition. Many of the new activities help students with the process of preparing and improving their speeches. The text now offers more peer evaluation activities, as well as additional material and activities on the following areas of **speech preparation:**

- analyzing the audience

- choosing appropriate topics

- organizing and outlining content by chronological order, main ideas, and logical argumentation

- supporting ideas with appropriate evidence such as statistics, examples, and quotations

- paraphrasing and summarizing the ideas of others

- choosing evidence to support a position

- preparing effective introductions and conclusions

- linking ideas within a speech and from speaker to speaker

- distinguishing between spoken and written English

Many activities have been added to provide practice in the following **delivery** skills:

- controlling volume, pausing, and rate of speaking

- improving eye contact, vitality, and posture

- establishing rapport with the audience

- using note cards and outlines

- using visual aids effectively

For students who need help with pronunciation, we have kept the original material in the appendix on rate, pauses, phrase grouping, and emphasis, and we have added new material for practice. We have also kept the original material on the final *s,* the final *ed,* word stress, and use of the dictionary to determine pronunciation.

As in the first edition, the book promotes the development of effective oral communication for more than just formal presentations. The communication contexts covered in the text include the following:

- *Interpersonal:* including giving encouragement, asking for additional information, asking for repetition or clarification, restating, interrupting, expressing agreement and disagreement, and using appropriate register

- *Small group:* including discussing topics and preparing presentations on them, evaluating portions of peers' presentations in preparation, practicing introductions and conclusions, evaluating supporting ideas, and evaluating speech organization

- *Large group:* including discussing ideas in dialogs and readings, reviewing course material, evaluating topics, critiquing model presentations and speech outlines, and preparing for and responding to questions from the audience

To complement the students' training in speaking skills, the book provides activities to develop students' listening skills. Appearing throughout the book are focused listening activities, such as listening to introductions and conclusions to evaluate their effectiveness. In addition, each unit features a global listening activity, the evaluation of a presentation. Revised evaluation forms are included in every unit and are designed to be used by instructors as well as students.

The readings and related exercises that introduced each unit in the first edition have been eliminated. Instead, units are introduced in a variety of ways, such as with dialogs, model speeches, and readings directly related to the speech assignment of the unit. Discussion questions focus on features of this introductory material as well as on the other content.

This book is accompanied by an instructor's manual that offers suggestions for overall course organization as well as for using the material effectively. It also contains material for listening activities, suggestions for additional activities, and copies of the evaluation forms for reproduction. This manual should benefit both ESL teachers and speech teachers. For a copy, please contact your local Wadsworth field representative or write to Angela Gantner, Wadsworth Publishing Company, 10 Davis Drive, Belmont, CA 94002.

Here it is our privilege and pleasure to thank all those students at San Francisco State University whose cooperation has facilitated the development and revision of this book. At the same time, we gratefully acknowledge the sage advice and careful editing of our mentor, Dorothy Danielson; the extensive assistance of colleagues Victoria Holder, Kate Kinsella, and Victoria Lasin; and the helpful suggestions of other colleagues, Jane Berger, Deborah Cohen, Andrea Kevech, Sandra McKay, Lyn Motai, Jay Schulman, Barry Taylor, and Elizabeth Whalley. We add special thanks to Pamela Gentile for content suggestions as well as her photographic skills. We would also like to thank Mercy Ho Charles for contributing the interview in Unit 2. Finally, we express our appreciation to Angela Gantner and Deborah Cogan at Wadsworth and to the following reviewers of our manuscript, who expended considerable time and effort and who offered many helpful suggestions: Christine Pearson Casanave, Stanford University; Vickie Christie, Eastern Montana College; O. Dean Gregory, University of Kansas; and Billy L. McClellan, El Paso Community College. We would like to give special acknowledgment to Nina T. Liakos, University of Maryland, for detailed comments that helped make this a better book.

COMMUNICATING
EFFECTIVELY
IN ENGLISH

Unit 1

Understanding Your Audience and Being Understood

INTRODUCTION

Have you ever found yourself in situations like these?

- You have many ideas to contribute to the discussion in your history class, but you never seem able to get into the discussion. On the one occasion when you did enter the discussion, no one seemed able to understand your idea.

- At the end of the lecture in your biology class, the professor gave an assignment. You didn't understand it but were too embarrassed to ask her to repeat it. After class you talked with some other non-native-speaking students in the class and found out that they didn't understand it either.

- You have just completed writing a computer program, and your supervisor has asked you to explain the applications of your program to a group of users. You are extremely worried about whether you can express your ideas clearly to them. Also, you are not sure how to organize such a demonstration.

- Your boss asked you to give a short oral presentation to the other members of your sales team. You wrote out the report very carefully, had someone check your grammar and pronunciation, and then read the report to the group. Your boss later told you he was very disappointed with your performance because you hadn't communicated the information well.

Can you describe other situations involving breakdowns in oral communication?

All these situations are common ones that non-native speakers of English (and native speakers of English) find themselves in, both at school and on the job. The source of difficulty in such situations may include the following:

- weak listening skills
- weak speaking skills
- a lack of confidence about speaking up to ask for clarification and/or help
- a lack of knowledge about the appropriate way to prepare and deliver a presentation
- a lack of experience in preparing and delivering a presentation

In this text we will work on solutions for such difficulties.

HOW DO YOU FEEL ABOUT COMMUNICATING?

Do you enjoy speaking in front of others in English? Do you like to talk to your classmates or co-workers individually but feel nervous when talking to a larger group? Just what are your feelings about communicating? Following are some statements from an attitude survey used to measure how college students who are native speakers of English feel about communicating. It is called a "communication anxiety" report because it measures the extent to which people feel worried and uneasy about speaking. By completing this survey you will have a chance to explore your own feelings about communicating. Also you will have a basis for comparing your feelings about communicating with those of your classmates, if you choose to do so.

Personal Report of Communication Anxiety*

Following are sixteen statements concerning feelings about communicating with other people. Indicate how the statements apply to you by marking whether each statement is ALWAYS true, OFTEN true, true HALF OF THE TIME, OCCASIONALLY true, or NEVER true. Circle the number under the

---

* Adapted from "Measures of Communication-Bound Anxiety," *Speech Monographs* 37(4), 1970, p. 272. Reprinted by permission of the Speech Communication Association and James C. McCroskey.

appropriate word(s). Work quickly: just record your first impression. Ask about any vocabulary that you don't understand. Respond to each statement with reference to speaking *in English,* not in your native language.

	ALWAYS	OFTEN	HALF OF THE TIME	OCCASIONALLY	NEVER
1. I enjoy facing an audience.	1	2	3	4	5
2. I look forward to expressing my opinion at meetings.	1	2	3	4	5
3. I look forward to an opportunity to speak in public.	1	2	3	4	5
4. I find the prospect of speaking to a large group mildly pleasant.	1	2	3	4	5
5. I feel that I am more fluent when talking to people than most other people are.	1	2	3	4	5
6. Although I am nervous just before getting up to speak, I soon forget my fears and enjoy the experience.	1	2	3	4	5
7. I feel relaxed while speaking to an audience.	1	2	3	4	5
8. I would enjoy presenting a speech on a local television show.	1	2	3	4	5
9. I try to avoid speaking in public.	5	4	3	2	1
10. I am fearful and tense while speaking before a group.	5	4	3	2	1
11. While participating in a conversation with a new acquaintance, I feel very nervous.	5	4	3	2	1
12. Although I talk fluently with friends, I am at a loss for words in front of an audience.	5	4	3	2	1
13. Conversing with people who hold positions of authority makes me fearful and tense.	5	4	3	2	1
14. I dislike using my body and voice expressively.	5	4	3	2	1

	ALWAYS	OFTEN	HALF OF THE TIME	OCCASIONALLY	NEVER
15. I am tense and nervous while participating in group discussions.	5	4	3	2	1
16. I feel self-conscious when called upon to answer a question or give an opinion in class.	5	4	3	2	1

Look back over the numbers you have circled. Note that statements 1–8 state positive feelings about communicating and statements 9–16 state negative feelings about communicating. Do you see any pattern to your responses? For example, if you have circled many low numbers (1s and 2s), this suggests that you are confident about speaking and have what can be called "low communication anxiety." If your numbers are consistently high (4s and 5s), then you may be somewhat anxious about communicating. You may find other patterns to your numbers: for example, you may be quite confident about speaking in small groups but lack confidence when speaking to a large audience (see statement 12), or you may feel comfortable when speaking in a classroom discussion (see statements 15 and 16) but not when standing up in front of an audience (see statements 9 and 10).

For Discussion

1. What are you most afraid of? According to surveys, speaking before a group is what Americans fear most—more than snakes, heights, disease, financial problems, or even death.* These surveys show that 85 percent feel "uncomfortably anxious" speaking in public. Discuss how you and your classmates rated on the anxiety survey, comparing your results for speaking in small groups, in the classroom, and in front of an audience. Do 85 percent of the students feel uncomfortable about public speaking?

2. What are some of the *costs* of speaking in front of an audience? For example, some costs students frequently cite are these: strangers can

---

* Michael T. Motley, "Taking the Terror Out of Talk," *Psychology Today,* January 1988, p. 46.

stare at you; you feel like an idiot when speaking; the audience is bored; your mind goes blank; your face gets red. What are some of the *benefits*? For example, you get others to listen to your ideas; you gain self-confidence that extends to other areas; you learn to speak more clearly. As a class or in small groups, come up with a list of costs and a list of benefits. Then discuss how the benefits may well outweigh the costs.

LEARNING ABOUT YOUR AUDIENCE

However you feel about communicating, one way to feel more confident and be more successful when speaking in any situation is to know your audience. The following activity and the assignment for this unit will enable you to learn more about your audience for this course—your classmates. In the coming months these classmates will be a constant source of help to you as you work to increase your speaking and listening skills. In addition, they will be a source of information and opinions as you collectively discuss ideas related to the various topics you choose to speak about.

Activity 1:   Getting Acquainted with Your Classmates

Brainstorm and come up with several topics (six to eight) that people in the class are interested in (for example, sports, politics, music, math, computer science, part-time jobs). At least two people should express interest in a given topic. The instructor will designate areas of the room where each topic may be discussed.

1. Select a topic you are interested in and then go to the appropriate area. Talk to the other students in your area about why you have chosen this topic, letting them know what in particular interests you about this topic.

2. After about ten minutes, *half* the members in each group should go to an area where a topic they are *not* particularly interested in is being discussed. In the newly formed groups, talk about why you are or are not enthusiastic about this topic.

3. Meet again as a whole class in a large circle. Each student should report on one thing he or she learned from these discussions *or* on a reaction to the discussions. For example, a student might report, "In the music

group, I found that I was the only one who doesn't play an instrument. Lots of my classmates like music because they play the piano or the guitar." A reaction might be, "I was pleased to meet other students who have the same major as mine. Two of them are taking the same accounting class as I am and we're going to form a study group."

ASSIGNMENT: GATHERING AND REPORTING INFORMATION ABOUT YOUR CLASSMATES

This assignment involves surveying your classmates and reporting on the results in a subsequent class period. For this assignment you need to do the following:

1. Brainstorm and come up with a list of ten to fifteen questions to find out information you would like to know about your future audience, that is, your classmates. For example, you might be interested in the ethnic background of your classmates; in their age range, family size, and length of time in the United States; in their majors, jobs, hobbies, and involvement in extracurricular activities; in their attitudes or opinions about particular issues; or in their scores on the communication anxiety survey.

2. Work in teams of two or three. Each team takes a different set of related questions. Then, using a list of classmates' names, survey each member of the class, asking your question or questions. (You can do the surveys individually, or you can work in teams.)

3. Prepare a summary of the results of your survey to present to the class. Both/all members of the team should participate in the brief presentation—that is, each member should report part of your results. The rest of the class should take notes on these presentations. The following sections give suggestions on organizing and presenting your information.

PREPARING YOUR REPORT

In preparing your report, you should break the task down into several steps: organizing the report, preparing visual aids, and preparing note cards.

Know your audience. Surveying your classmates to find out about their interests and attitudes will help you become a more confident and successful speaker.

Organizing Your Report

A sensible way to organize the presentation of your report is as follows:

SPEAKER 1:   introduction

survey results

transition to partner

SPEAKER 2:   transition from partner

survey results

conclusion

Here are some tips to help you develop each part of your presentation.

Introduction   Here, you want to introduce yourself and your partner and tell when you did this survey, why you did it, and what you wanted to find out.

> EXAMPLE: Good afternoon. My name is X, and this is my partner,
> Y. Last class, we asked all of you what your nationality was and
> how long you had been in this country. We were particularly in-
> terested in these questions because when we looked around the
> room, it seemed that everyone was from the same part of the world,
> that is, from Asia. Also it seemed to us that most of the class spoke
> English really well, and this suggested that many of you had been
> here quite a long time.

Results   Begin by restating the topic you are responsible for. Then give the results, supplying as much detail as possible.

> EXAMPLE: Now I'd like to present the results of our first question
> about nationalities. We have discovered that 23 of our 25 class-
> mates are Asian; 15 are from Hong Kong, 5 are from Indonesia,
> and 3 are from Japan; the 2 non-Asians are from . . .

Transitions   Once the first speaker is finished, he or she needs to make a transition to the next speaker to show the audience the connection between what each speaker is reporting. For clarity and continuity, the next speaker can briefly restate what the first speaker has said before discussing additional results in detail.

> EXAMPLE
>
> SPEAKER 1:   Now that you know more about where our classmates are
> from, my partner, Y, will tell you what we learned about
> their length of residence in the United States.
>
> SPEAKER 2:   Thank you, X. As X has said, the majority of the students
> in the class turned out to be from Asia, as we had guessed.
> But for our other question, the length of time in the United
> States, the results were somewhat surprising. First of all, we
> found a wide variety of lengths of time . . .

Conclusion   Finally, after you have reported all your information, you must conclude your presentation. Here, it would be appropriate to comment on how you felt about talking to your classmates and/or the results you gathered. Also, you might want to end on an upbeat note by expressing positive hopes for future interaction with your classmates.

> EXAMPLE: We have discovered that some members of our class
> have lived in this country for quite a long time; we hope that those
> students can help the rest of us when we have trouble with cul-

tural problems. Both my partner and I enjoyed talking to you and look forward to working with you this semester.

To end your report effectively, keep your energy level and your volume high throughout your conclusion. In wrapping up, avoid expressions such as "That's it" or "That's all"; such comments sound apologetic and inappropriate. If you want to say something more, a simple "Thank you" would be better.

Preparing Visual Aids

For your presentation it may be helpful to summarize your results in a chart or a graph. Such visual aids not only can make what you have to say more comprehensible to your audience, they can make it more interesting as well. You could prepare your visual on a large poster or on a transparency to be

Use visual aids such as a bar graph to make the results of your survey both clear and interesting.

Figure 1.1   Visual Aids

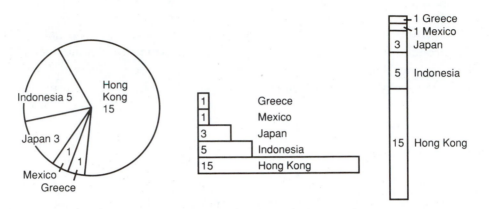

used with an overhead projector. Or you could draw it on the chalkboard, putting it on the board before class starts if it takes more than a few seconds to draw. For the sample report on nationalities, the results could easily be presented in either a pie chart or a bar graph. Figure 1.1 shows three possibilities.

Preparing Note Cards

After you and your partner have worked out what you want to say in your report, you need to put that information on note cards for effective delivery. Your note cards should contain notes, *not* complete sentences. This way, you will not be tempted to read your speech. Even though you will have only a few note cards for this presentation, it is a good idea to number them in case they accidentally get out of order. Your notes should be large enough to read at a glance. Also, you should put just one or two points on a card. Look at the two sample note cards in Figure 1.2 and decide which one you would rather speak from and why.

DELIVERING YOUR REPORT

A presentation has two important components: *what* you say (the content) and *how* you say it (the delivery). The term **delivery** covers a wide range of features of speaking. There are physical elements, such as posture, gestures, eye contact, voice control (volume, rate), and comprehensibility; and speaking

Figure 1.2 Note Cards

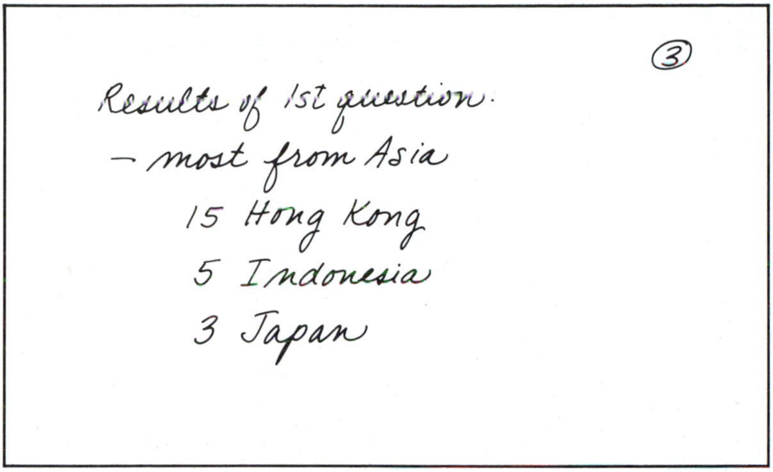

③

Results of 1st question.
— most from Asia
 15 Hong Kong
 5 Indonesia
 3 Japan

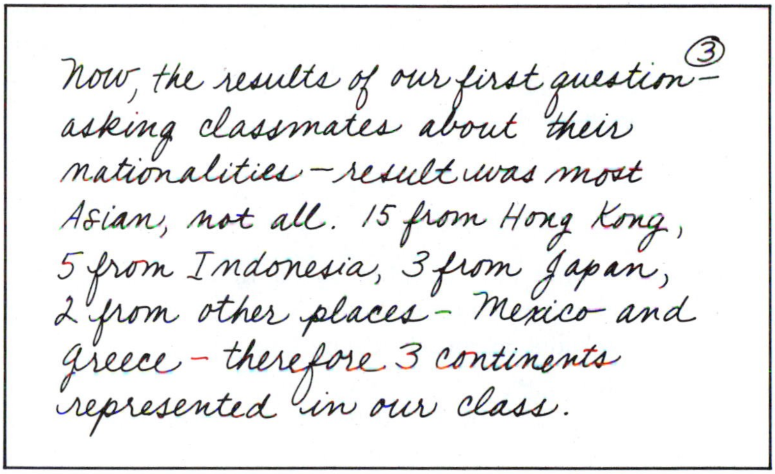

③

Now, the results of our first question —
asking classmates about their
nationalities — result was most
Asian, not all. 15 from Hong Kong,
5 from Indonesia, 3 from Japan,
2 from other places — Mexico and
greece — therefore 3 continents
represented in our class.

dynamics, such as vitality, confidence, spontaneity, use of humor, and interaction with the audience. Of course, it is difficult, if not impossible, to think of what you are saying, as well as to pay attention to all the features of delivery, at the same time. To help you prepare for your first speech and for all your other speeches, this section will introduce you to all the elements of speech delivery. The activities in this section will give you some practice with these elements and will give you some idea of which elements you will need to work on further as the course progresses.

Nervousness

It is the rare speaker who can get up and address an audience without any feelings of nervousness. Most people feel varying degrees of nervousness in this situation, especially the first time they talk to an audience the size of an average class. Indeed, some teachers may feel nervous about meeting a new class of students for the first time. Do most people eventually overcome their nervous feelings? Usually not, but they do learn to control their nervousness so that it is almost imperceptible to the audience.

What should you do about your nervousness? Well, of course, the first way you can increase your confidence is by being really well prepared. You should try to make sure that your topic is interesting, your material is well organized, and your delivery has been improved through practice. Another way to reduce nervousness is to focus more on the message you want to get across than on the fact that you are standing alone in front of a room with a lot of people looking at you. Finally, remember that your fellow students all have to undergo the same experience; therefore, on the whole, they are more likely to be supportive than critical. Although you may not believe it now, you will find that by the time you give your last speech, you will have made considerable improvement in controlling your nervousness.

Posture

Posture is the way you hold your body, whether sitting or standing. Usually, when you give a speech, you will be standing. You should look alert and stand reasonably erect, but with relaxed posture. If you look too stiff, it will turn off your audience; on the other hand, if you slouch with your hands in your pockets, it will look as if you don't care. Nervousness may tend to make you hold yourself stiffly at first, but your posture should improve as you learn to relax.

Movement

A certain amount of movement while giving a speech can be helpful, although it is not always necessary. Taking a few steps forward or to one side can help emphasize a point you are making. However, you need to guard against rocking back and forth, shifting from one foot to the other, and wandering aimlessly about—all of which can prove distracting.

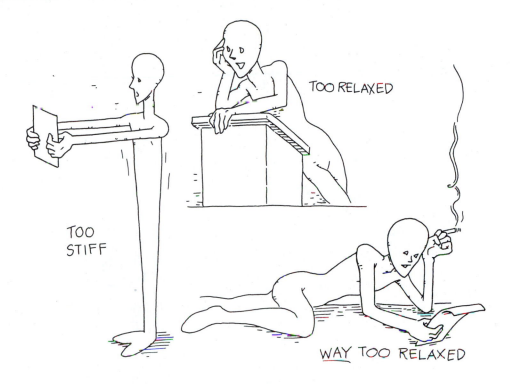

When you speak, you should look alert and stand
reasonably erect, but with relaxed posture.

Facial Expression and Gestures

A smile as you begin your speech can give an impression of friendliness but should not be forced if it does not come naturally. On the other hand, too much smiling is not a good idea, as it usually seems insincere. Like smiling, the use of gestures (hand and arm movements) is a reflection of personality. But gestures can be very helpful in conveying meaning, especially when they are used to indicate size or direction. Preachers and politicians sometimes thump the podium or table when they want to emphasize a point. Thus, gestures used in moderation can add vitality to a speech, but again, overuse results in distraction. Distracting gestures to avoid are flipping your hair off your face, scratching your head or your chin, folding your arms, fiddling with a pen, pencil, piece of chalk, and so on.

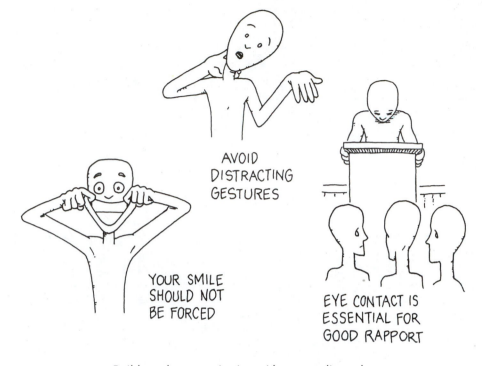

AVOID
DISTRACTING
GESTURES

YOUR SMILE
SHOULD NOT
BE FORCED

EYE CONTACT IS
ESSENTIAL FOR
GOOD RAPPORT

Build good communication with your audience by
using appropriate facial expressions,
gestures, and eye contact.

Eye Contact

The appropriate use of eye contact varies from one culture to another. In some cultures, women are expected to lower their eyes in most communication settings; in others, younger people must keep their eyes lowered when addressing older people. However, in the United States, whether you are addressing an individual, a small group of people, or a larger audience, you are expected to look at them. You do not have to stare intensely and continuously; in fact, it is appropriate when speaking to one person to look away occasionally. In a small group you should look around at the different members of the group. And when addressing a larger audience, you should try to make eye contact with different people around the room. It is important to look at the entire audience, not just the people in the center of the room, so you will probably have to turn your head and/or your body in order to make proper eye contact with people seated at the sides of the room. If you look at the floor or the ceiling or out of the window, you will give the impression that you are not interested in your topic or in your audience and their reactions to what you have to say. A speaker establishes rapport with the audience mainly through eye contact, and good rapport is essential to the success of any speech.

Vitality

Vitality is a combination of liveliness and enthusiasm. Obviously you will be more vital and lively if you are talking about a subject you feel interested in and enthusiastic about. An audience usually can tell right away whether you care about the subject you are presenting. If you are not interested in your topic, all the areas of speech delivery will probably be affected. Your posture may be bad, you will use few if any gestures, and your voice will probably be flat. On the other hand, presenting a topic you are enthusiastic about and want to share with others will inevitably result in a more lively appearance, more spontaneous gestures, and better voice quality, all characteristics of a good speaker.

Spontaneity

A good speaker also talks directly to the audience, rather than reading the speech or speaking from memory. This quality of speaking in a natural manner rather than repeating previously planned exact words is called *spontaneity*. Of course, professional actresses and actors are skilled at making memorized lines sound spontaneous, but most other people are not. For your presentations, you can rely on your notes for the points you want to cover and make up the actual sentences as you speak. This means you will probably use different wording each time you practice, and the wording in your actual speech will also differ somewhat from that of your final practice. Such an approach is necessary if you want to sound spontaneous.

Sense of Humor

Being able to use humor at appropriate times during a presentation is a great asset to a speaker. Even in a speech about a very serious topic, a humorous remark or anecdote can help establish a bond between you and your audience. Because the use of humor can vary from one culture to another, it would be a good idea for you to pay attention to how humor is used in American culture. Then you can experiment with including a bit of humor in your speeches. Before actually giving your speech, you might try out your humorous remarks on a classmate or two or on a native speaker of English: this will give you an idea of whether your humor "works"—that is, whether your remarks sound natural, appropriate, and indeed humorous.

Voice Control

Learning to exercise good voice control is also very important if you are to become an effective speaker. Voice control entails a number of elements, including the following:

- **Rate** refers to the speed at which you speak. The main criterion for your rate of speech is that you be easy to understand. If you speak too fast, you will lose and frustrate your audience, and if you speak too slowly, you will bore them. Many people tend to speak too fast when they are nervous; therefore, if you have this tendency, try to slow down. For suggestions on improving your speech rate, see the "Rate of Speech" section in the Appendix.

- **Fluency** refers to speaking smoothly with as few hesitations as possible. Although everyone at times hesitates in order to gather his or her thoughts, fillers such as "mm," "er," "ah," "OK," and "you know" can be very distracting. Fluency is also affected by pauses, phrase grouping, and emphasis. If you pause in unexpected places and emphasize words or syllables not normally stressed in the context in which you are using them, you will have difficulty being understood. Refer to the "Pauses and Phrase Grouping" and "Emphasis" sections in the Appendix.

- **Volume** refers to the loudness or softness with which you speak. You should use sufficient volume so that everyone in the room can hear you without difficulty. This may mean that you have to talk louder to adjust to noise outside the classroom, such as students talking in the hall or mowers running outside the window.

- **Intonation** refers to the variations in pitch of words and syllables: some words or syllables are said on a higher pitch and some on a lower pitch. Just as music has rises and falls in pitch, so our speech has a "melody"; it is this melody that is called intonation. For instance, in English we usually raise the pitch on the last words of a yes/no question such as

"Is John here?" and lower the pitch on the last words of a statement such as "He left an hour ago." Accenting a word or syllable with a pitch that is higher or lower than the one before it makes that word or syllable stand out: it gives you a way to emphasize certain information because it is important or new. Thus, proper intonation is essential to getting your message across.

Being able to *vary* your volume, rate, and intonation is important to achieve maximum expressiveness. A speech delivered in a monotone (no change in pitch), without change in volume or rate, is likely to put an audience to sleep. On the other hand, changing pace and volume at selected times can help engage your audience. The speaking assignment on page 226 in the Appendix provides practice in rate, pausing, emphasis, and volume, all important components of voice control.

Comprehensibility

Your comprehensibility—that is, how well your audience can understand what you are saying—depends partly on the voice control factors of rate, fluency, volume, and intonation. Your comprehensibility also depends on your **pronunciation,** that is, the way you articulate the sounds of English. The focus of this book does not allow time for intensive pronunciation practice; however, the Appendix does contain information on and practice in two important problem areas: final *s* and final *ed*. It also provides information on and practice in using the dictionary to determine pronunciation of correct sounds, word stress, and word stress patterns.

It is a good idea to consult the dictionary for the pronunciation of any words you are unfamiliar with. Also, before giving your presentation, it is essential to go over the pronunciation of *key words* with your instructor or a native English-speaking friend to make absolutely sure you know how to pronounce them correctly. The audience may not understand any of your speech if you mispronounce the key words. Don't make the mistake of the speaker who confused his audience with a three-minute talk on "snake machines" because he didn't know how to pronounce the word *snack* correctly.

For Discussion

1. What experiences have you had with nervousness as a speaker? What strategies have you found successful in dealing with nervousness? Which of the suggestions in the text do you think will be helpful to you in making your presentations in this class?

2. What impression do you get from a speaker who slouches and leans on the table or the speaker's podium? From a speaker who moves aimlessly back and forth while speaking?

3. What are the customs regarding eye contact in cultures you are familiar with, and how do they differ from the rules in American culture? You might describe the rules for eye contact between younger and older people, between people of the same age but opposite sex, or between people of greater and lesser power status (for example, a boss and employee, a teacher and student). Do the rules differ depending on whether you are speaking or listening?

4. How would you describe a person who speaks with vitality? What is the effect on you as a listener if a speaker has no vitality?

5. Why is it important to speak in a spontaneous manner? What can you do to ensure that your delivery is characterized by spontaneity?

6. How does occasional use of humor contribute to an effective presentation? Can you describe situations in which humor is used differently in American culture than in another culture?

7. What are the elements of voice control? What are some steps you can take to improve your voice control for public speaking?

8. If one audience member says to another, "The last speaker talked with wonderful vitality, but the speech was simply incomprehensible," what does the audience member mean? What elements of comprehensibility do you feel you need to work on?

Activity 2: Relaxing to Control Nervousness

Although it is unrealistic to think that you can control all nervousness when you give a presentation, you can use the following routine to relax yourself before beginning to speak. The whole routine can be done while seated. Practice it daily for a few weeks—at your desk or while watching TV—so that you can apply it automatically in moments of stress. After doing this exercise in class, discuss other techniques you are familiar with—either physical or mental—that help reduce anxiety and nervousness.

1. Sit on a fairly hard chair.

2. To get rid of tension in your body, do the following:

   a. Stretch your arms out to your sides, up over your head, and back down.

   b. Move your head from side to side; then move it forward and down and then back; finally, move it back to a position where your chin is parallel to the floor.

   c. Stretch out your legs in front of you, flex your toes toward you, then point them away; flex them again and put your feet back down on the floor.

   d. Stretch your upper body up as high as you can, inhale, and as you exhale twist to the right; come back to center, stretch up and inhale again, and as you exhale twist to the left.

3. Get comfortable in your chair while remaining alert. Sit as far back in the chair as you can. Relax your hands, palms up, in your lap. Keep your spine straight, relax your shoulders, and keep your head level. Feel the chair supporting you.

4. Close your eyes and lower your head. Take two normal breaths and then on the third breath exhale slowly, deeply, and steadily. Do not strain or force the breath. Maintain your posture.

5. Continue inhaling normally but drawing out every third exhalation. After three to five minutes, resume breathing normally, and then lift your head and open your eyes. You should feel calm and alert.

Activity 3: *Using Gestures for Expressiveness*

Each person will receive a slip of paper with an adjective describing an emotion written on it. *Don't let anyone else see your word.* Now, you'll have thirty seconds to consider what that emotion is like and how you will act it out. Form small groups of five or six and arrange your chairs in a line. Then,

Gestures communicate. They add to your expressiveness
and vitality as a speaker.

one at a time, a group member should stand up in front of the group and act
out that emotion using facial expressions and gestures *only*. The person who
is "on" must continuously act out that feeling for fifteen seconds. Then other
members can try to guess which emotion is being acted out.

Here are the emotions found on the slips:

angry	embarrassed	happy	nervous
annoyed	excited	hopeful	sad
ashamed	frightened	lonely	surprised
bored	frustrated	loving	thoughtful

If time permits, your group may wish to briefly discuss this question: How do
facial expressions and gestures reflecting these emotions vary from culture to
culture?

Activity 4: *Speaking Spontaneously and Maintaining Eye Contact*

This exercise will help you get the feel of just talking without receiving any verbal feedback from your "audience." It will give you the opportunity to speak spontaneously on one topic for a brief period of time and to practice looking at your partner.

1. Arrange the classroom chairs in two lines so that there are an equal number of chairs in each line. (Or arrange the chairs in two concentric circles, with the chairs in the inner circle facing the chairs in the outer circle.)

2. The students in one line (or on the inside chairs) will talk about a topic provided by the instructor for approximately two minutes, with each speaker addressing the listener directly opposite, looking at the listener from time to time. The listener should nod, look at the speaker, and show interest (and can give verbal signals such as "uh-huh") but should not talk.

3. At the end of two minutes, the speakers should all move to the next seat so that they will have new listeners. This time they will talk on the same topic for a minute and a half.

4. Now the two lines (or circles) reverse roles. The instructor will give a new topic, and the former listeners will be the speakers, first for two minutes, then for a minute and a half, with two different listeners.

5. Discuss these points:

   a. Was it easy to make eye contact when you were the speaker? When you were the listener? Why or why not?

   b. Did you have trouble thinking of what to say? Why or why not?

   c. How was the second "round" of talking (the shorter period of time) different from the first?

   d. What did you like best—being a speaker or a listener?

Activity 5:   *Looking Up from Your Notes*

For oral presentations most experienced speakers use note cards, but they do not forget to look up at the audience. To give you practice in looking at your audience when using notes, do this quick exercise.

Form pairs and stand facing your partner, at least four feet apart. Your instructor will give you each a note card containing three or four sentence cues that you will use to form questions. One partner begins: glance at your card for a second, and then look up at your partner and ask a complete question suggested by the first cue on the card. For example, if the cue on the card is "time at this school," the speaker could ask, "How long have you been a student here at this school?" Your partner will watch to make sure you do not look down again at the card. If you succeed, you may go on to the next cue on your card. If not, try the first one again. After one partner has asked all his or her questions, reverse roles.

Activity 6:   Working on Vitality

In pairs, take turns acting out the following situation: You have just run into a good friend whom you haven't seen for several weeks. Your friend says, "So, tell me what's new with you." You tell your friend about something that you are really excited about or happy about that has happened to you recently.

Before you begin your description, take a moment to reflect quietly on what you will say. Then, as you talk, do your best to be lively and enthusiastic. Put as much energy into your conversation as you can. Don't worry if this outgoing and lively person isn't "the real you." Get into it and enjoy the energy you and your partner generate.

Activity 7:   Working on Volume, Rate, Posture, and Eye Contact

This activity will give you a feel for creating sentences from notes, as well as give you an idea about how big or small your writing should be. You will get help with your volume, rate, posture, and eye contact from your instructor and your classmates.

Arrange the classroom chairs in a circle. Each student should take a three-by-five note card and write one word on the card for each of three topics, using different size print. Possible topics and sizes are a city (normal handwriting size), food (bigger handwriting), and an activity (still bigger). Each student should exchange cards with a partner across the circle.

Each student should stand up, face the group, and make up connected sentences using the cue words. (For example, with the words *Jakarta, rice,* and *jogging,* the student might say, "Last summer I took a trip to Jakarta, the capital city of Indonesia. While I was there, I ate a lot of rice. Of course, I eat a lot of rice at home, too. Unfortunately, it was too hot for me to go jogging, which is my favorite activity.") By looking at the three sizes of handwriting, the speaker can decide which size is best for future note cards.

As each participant speaks, the instructor will provide coaching on volume, eye contact, posture, and the way the student holds the cards. The rest of the class should ask for clarification, repetition, increased volume, or slower speed, as necessary (for example, "Please speak louder. I can't hear you at all" or "Would you talk a little slower and repeat that, please?").

Each student should fill out a simple feedback form for his or her partner as the partner is speaking, then give it to the partner when everyone has spoken. Here's an example of what the form might look like:

	EXCELLENT	OKAY	A PROBLEM
Volume	_____	_____	_____
Rate	_____	_____	_____
Posture	_____	_____	_____
Eye contact	_____	_____	_____

For additional practice, do this activity again using a topic assigned by your instructor. Some suggested topics are an ideal day, an ideal vacation, an ideal house (apartment, date, friend, car, teacher, job, class, and so on). This time, prepare your own notes to speak from; don't exchange with a partner. For example, for an ideal day, you might make notes on where you would be, what you would do, who you would be with, and so on. Your notes should be words or phrases, not sentences, and written big enough to see easily. Speak for about one minute.

Partners can again evaluate each other. The person on the evaluator's left should be prepared to ask the speaker a question at the end of the speech.

LISTENING TO AND EVALUATING THE REPORTS

As you speak and as you listen to your classmates speak, you need to pay attention to both the content and the delivery of the presentation. For this first report we suggest that you focus on three areas of content (as indicated in the following evaluation form): the introduction or conclusion, the information in the report, and the transition to or from the other speaker. In terms of delivery, you should focus on volume, rate, comprehensibility, posture, and eye contact. Your instructor will give you a copy of the form and will assign you a classmate to evaluate. The instructor will also use this form to evaluate you. The evaluations will give you an idea about what you are doing well and what you need to work on in future presentations.

Unit 1   Report on Survey

Speaker _____

Evaluator _____

Topic _____

RATING SYSTEM: + = excellent
                  √ = average
                  − = weak

Content

_____ Introduction (or conclusion)

_____ Information

_____ Transition to/from other speaker

Delivery

_____ Volume

_____ Rate

_____ Comprehensibility

_____ Posture

_____ Eye contact

Suggestions for next presentation:

Unit 2

Getting Information:
Interviews and Conferences

SAMPLE INTERVIEW

Rita and Anna are students in an oral communication class who recently met each other for the first time. Rita is going to interview Anna and then give a report of her interview to the class. Anna suggested the topic of the interview during the last class period.

RITA: Hi Anna! How're you doing?

ANNA: I'm fine, thanks. But I feel kind of overloaded with school-work at the moment.

RITA: Me too! I know how you feel. Well, maybe we should get started with the interview. Before we get to the main topic, I'd like to get some general information for my report. Is that OK?

ANNA: Sure.

RITA: Your family name is Ng, right? Spelled *N–G*?

ANNA: Right.

RITA: I think you told me you're from Taiwan? And how long have you been here?

ANNA: Yes, I'm from Taiwan, and I've been here about two years.

RITA: Thanks. And now, you said we could discuss a problem you had when you first came to the U.S. Would you like to start telling me about your problem?

ANNA: Yes, of course. You see, when I first left Taiwan, I went to New York, and I studied at the City University for one semester. Anyway—I had this friend from Taiwan, who had moved to an area just outside New York, so I thought I'd look her up.

RITA: Was it a problem finding her?

ANNA: No. That wasn't the problem.

RITA: Oh, sorry for interrupting. Please go on.

ANNA: Well, one Saturday, I bought a map, and I got on the subway. I rode for what seemed like a long time, and I finally found my way to her place. She was my best friend in elementary school, but her family moved to the States just after we transferred to junior high school. I was really looking forward to seeing her again, and I imagined that she'd be happy to see me too. But that wasn't what happened!

RITA: I guess she was out when you got there, huh?

ANNA: No, she was home all right. But the first thing she said to me was, "Why didn't you let me know you were coming?"

RITA: I can imagine how that made you feel. What on earth did you say?

ANNA: Well, I asked her if something was wrong, and she told me straight out that people here usually call before they visit. She said if I'd called first, she could have arranged to have more free time.

RITA: That was pretty blunt of her. Poor you! What happened after that?

ANNA: She made some tea and we talked for a while, but I felt bad all the time I was there. I was quite relieved when she offered to drive me back to the station.

RITA: That was really too bad. Did you hear from her after that?

ANNA: Well, I moved to San Francisco a little while after that. We've written a couple of letters since then, I guess.

RITA: And how do you feel about the incident now?

ANNA: Well, I understand her attitude better now. You see, after people live here for a while, they start to adopt the American lifestyle themselves. Actually it's happened to me. Recently I've had hardly any free time to spend with my friends. I suppose it's just natural to start to follow the ways of the culture you live in.

RITA: I guess you're right. Do you think there's anything people can do to avoid getting caught in the type of situation you found yourself in?

ANNA: Um. I'm not really sure. But it wouldn't hurt to learn as much as possible about the lifestyle in the U.S. before they come here.

RITA: But how do you think they could do this?

ANNA: Well, they could talk to their friends who've been to the U.S. . . . and they could watch American TV programs . . . and maybe read some articles or books.

RITA: Yeah, those sound like pretty good ideas to me. Well, thanks for the interview. You never know—learning about your experience might help some of our classmates.

ANNA: You're welcome. Good luck with your report!

For Discussion

1. Which questions do you think Rita prepared before her interview with Anna? Were they good questions? Can you think of others she might have prepared?

2. Which questions does Rita use to get Anna to continue her story?

3. When and why does Rita interrupt Anna? Does the interruption seem polite?

4. When and how does Rita show empathy for Anna?

5. How does Rita end the interview? Does it seem like a good ending?

6. What cultural problems did you encounter when you first came to the United States? How did you feel about them at the time they occurred? How do you feel about them now? What advice could you give to new-comers to avoid these problems?

7. Have you ever been interviewed? Have you ever interviewed anyone? Tell about your experiences.

COMMUNICATING

What is communicating, and why do we communicate? According to Rudolph F. Verderber, author of several books on communication, **communication** is sharing meaning. The word *sharing* is of key importance and indicates why communication is basic to human society. People must communicate—share meaning—in order to establish relationships and accomplish tasks. At least two people must interact with each other for sharing to take place. This interaction involves sending, receiving, and responding to messages, which may be verbal (that is, spoken) or nonverbal (for instance, nodding your head to show that you are listening to what is being said). When communicating with others, you have responsibilities both as a speaker and as a listener, and the more actively you are able to perform these roles, the more successful you are likely to be—in school and in life.

Being an Active Speaker

As a student, you may think of yourself as primarily a listener, but successful students put effort into both listening and speaking. At the beginning of a course, it is important to find out exactly what the teacher expects of students. At home you can carefully study the information sheets that the teacher hands out, but in class you must be an active listener to make sure that you can understand and follow the course requirements. If you do not understand something, then you must change your role from listener to speaker by raising your hand and asking for clarification of whatever is not clear. Although students in some countries may rarely ask questions in class, American teachers consider it the student's responsibility to seek clarification and will frequently pause to ask if students have any questions. Some teachers may even regard students who never ask questions as disinterested or lazy.

In all your classes you will probably have questions. Rather than sitting silently, you should try to speak up and ask them; in this way you will gain practice in speaking in a large group. Other students will almost certainly have the same questions and will feel grateful to you for asking. It is also considered more appropriate to ask relevant questions about class work during the class period than to ask the instructor after class. However, if you want to communicate about a personal matter, you may, of course, talk with your instructor before or after class or visit the instructor's office during office hours. Your classmates are another good source of information, so you should also make an effort to ask them questions about things you are not sure of and, in return, to respond to their questions.

If you are distracted by your own thoughts, you
won't be able to listen actively.

Being an Active Listener

What does it mean to be an active listener? It means that you focus both
physical and mental energy on what a speaker is saying. Merely sitting pas-
sively, hearing but not consciously attending, seriously limits your ability to
absorb and interpret information accurately. Active listening is the only way
to come close to understanding what a speaker is saying; it means paying attention not only to *what* is said but also to *how* it is said. Tone of voice, facial
expressions, and gestures can sometimes indicate more effectively how a
speaker feels about a subject than what he or she expresses verbally. In order
to receive both verbal and nonverbal messages clearly, you need to develop
good listening habits.

You need to take a positive attitude toward listening. Even though the
subject may be one that you are either unfamiliar with or have never felt moti-
vated to learn about, a good approach would be to try to find out as much
new information as you can. To help you concentrate, you could pretend that
you have to prepare a report on what is being said for someone who is not
present. For example, suppose you are listening to a speech on why it is better
to drink tap water than bottled water. Because you don't think this topic is
very interesting, to help yourself concentrate you decide to take notes to share
with some friends who always buy bottled water.

Sometimes you may find yourself so distracted by your own thoughts
that you don't really attend to what the speaker has to say. In this case you
need to try to put yourself in the speaker's shoes. Think how you would feel
if you were speaking and your audience didn't appear to be listening. As an

illustration, consider the case of a student named Harry, who is involved in a small-group discussion in which the members are helping one another prepare for their forthcoming speeches. Harry tells his group about his speech plans, and they listen carefully and make some helpful suggestions. But when it comes to listening to the other group members, Harry is still busy thinking about his own speech and thus is unable to help them with their speeches.

Do you sometimes pay attention to what others are saying but listen only for things you are already interested in and ignore everything else? If so, you are missing a great opportunity to expand your present knowledge and ideas. For example, suppose you find yourself listening to a speech about adopting a healthy lifestyle. You want to lose weight, so you listen to the part about diet, but you shut out the parts about using your car less and exercising more.

Some people listen only for points that they can argue about. This kind of listener often interrupts the speaker in order to provide his or her own point of view. It is usually better, however, to allow a speaker to finish expressing his or her point of view first. Hearing a speaker out is important in inter-personal conversations, in group discussions, and in public debates. By doing so, you may find that your grounds for disagreement are not as strong as you originally thought. And, in the end, if you still wish to express your disagreement, you will have a sounder basis for doing so than jumping in at the start. You may, for example, be a strong supporter of capital punishment, believing that it serves as a deterrent to crime. But if you hear a speaker provide some statistics showing that the crime rate is higher in those states that permit capital punishment than in those that don't, you must take this information into account when you make your response.

Do you become very upset if a speaker expresses a point of view different from yours? If so, it might be a good idea to look at your own attitudes and biases. It is important to remember that others may have different but equally valid values and beliefs based on their own experiences. For instance, in a group discussion about an international problem, one member who has never experienced war firsthand may advocate the use of force to settle the problem. Another member of the group who previously lived in a city that was bombed may speak passionately against the use of force—his home was destroyed, he lost family members and friends, and he had to struggle to survive after the attack. Each group member will have to make a special effort to understand the point of view of the other.

In addition to acknowledging the validity of points of view different from your own, you need to be sensitive to the emotions of those who speak to you. In American culture, making good eye contact with the speaker is one way of indicating that you are giving your full attention. Particularly in one-to-one conversations, you can provide a needed source of support, empathy, and encouragement to the person who is confiding in you, a role that can be uplifting to both listener and speaker. In the interview at the beginning of this unit, as Rita listens carefully to Anna tell of her bad experience, she empathizes by saying "Poor you!" and "That was too bad!" We would assume that, in these instances, Rita was listening closely to Anna and was observing the physical signs of her emotion; she was, therefore, very much aware of how Anna was feeling.

While you are working to improve your listening skills, it is also important to realize that, as a listener, you too are sending messages back to the speaker. If you look worried, the speaker may think you are upset about something. If you look at your book or out the window, the speaker will probably think you are bored. Therefore, as you listen, you must try to show interest in what the speaker is saying.

Besides taking a positive approach to listening, there are several steps you can take to help yourself listen actively:

1. Try to ignore outside noises.

2. Put books, magazines, papers, pens, and pencils that you are not actually using someplace where they will not prove a distraction.

3. Concentrate on what the speaker is saying and try not to think of anything else. We tend to become distracted because we can think much faster than a person can speak. Extra time can be used to watch for nonverbal cues and to take notes if appropriate.

4. Make eye contact with the speaker.

5. Be prepared to restate the speaker's main ideas.

6. Be prepared to offer feedback.

Finally, you will find that improving your listening skills can benefit you in a number of ways. By listening to *what* others have to say, you may learn things that you didn't know before, you will be able to compare your own views with those of others and to modify them when appropriate, and you will have opportunities to find out how others think and thus will understand them better. By paying attention to *how* others speak, you will be better able to interpret what they are saying, you will learn the effectiveness of gestures and facial expressions, and you will see the effect that speaker confidence or lack of it has on communication. These advantages make it well worth your while to become an effective, active listener.

For Discussion

1. Think of times when you have not paid attention to what others are saying. Describe one or two of those occasions. What was the cause of your lack of attention?

2. What kinds of topics do you think are boring—in conversations, in classes, in other situations?

3. What kinds of topics sometimes cause others to argue with you, or you with others?

4. On what occasions have you been surprised to find that someone you have been talking with has a different opinion from yours?

5. Have you ever felt better after just talking about a problem with someone? What was the listener's attitude?

6. As a speaker (in a conversation or in a class that requires you to speak), what kinds of listener behaviors do you find distracting or annoying?

7. What strategies do you use to help you listen with more concentration, say, during a lecture or in a class discussion?

8. What benefits have you experienced from being a good listener?

Activity 1:   Listening and Retelling a Story

Three or four students should volunteer to be active listeners. After all but one of them has left the room, the instructor will then tell a brief story to the remaining volunteer, who listens actively, along with the other members of the class. One of the students from outside then comes in, and the volunteer who previously listened to the story repeats it to the new active listener. That student repeats it to another from outside, and so on until all the volunteers have heard the story. The last student repeats the story to the class, and then the instructor gives the original version again. The class and the volunteer active listeners should be prepared to discuss what changed in the story and why as it passed from one listener to another.

Activity 2:   Listening and Taking Notes

1. As your instructor gives a short speech, listen and take notes on the points that seem important to you. Try to look up at the instructor from time to time during the speech.

2. Be prepared to compare your notes with those of your classmates and to discuss why you selected particular points.

3. Discuss how taking notes helped or hindered your ability to be an active listener.

INTERVIEWING AND PARTICIPATING IN A CONFERENCE

In this section we focus on how to conduct an interview and participate in a conference. In addition to learning when to use formal and informal language, you'll also learn how to prepare appropriate questions and how to elicit information spontaneously during the interview or conference. The assignments are (1) an interview with a classmate and an oral report of the interview and (2) a conference with an instructor or supervisor and a written report of the conference.

Choosing between Formal and Informal Language

The choice of whether to use formal or informal English depends on several factors: the people who are communicating, their relationship, the setting, the topic, and the occasion. The most formal spoken language is reserved for occasions like speeches at a university graduation ceremony. Furthermore, formal language is more likely to be used in speeches than in small-group discussions or conversation. For example, you probably wouldn't address your classmates as "you guys" in a speech to the whole class, but you might well address other members of a small group in this way.

In conversation the level of formality varies according to the participants and the situation in which they find themselves. For example, peers in informal settings generally use casual language. In contrast, a conversation between a teacher and a student is normally more formal than it is between two teachers or between two students who know each other well. Conversation between a teacher and a student is also likely to be more formal in the classroom or in the teacher's office when discussing class-related matters than it

Use language appropriate for the formality
of the situation.

would be over lunch in the cafeteria. Thus, the level of formality of the language you use in your interview with a classmate will probably be similar to the level you would use in a casual conversation, although you might want to use a more formal level with an older classmate. A conference with your instructor or supervisor will naturally call for more formal language than will the interview with your classmate.

Fortunately, you do not have to be overly concerned about levels of formality since most of the spoken language we use is rather neutral, that is, neither formal nor informal. Nevertheless, you need to be aware that certain expressions and forms of address can give the language a more formal or informal tone. For instance, "no way" is much more informal than "certainly not," and "hi" is more informal than "good morning. ' And once you become familiar with informal greetings such as "What's happening?" and "How's it going?" you may sometimes choose to use them with your peers, but it would be inappropriate to use them with your instructors. Also note that in the dialog at the beginning of the unit, Rita used the informal question "What on earth did you say?" when told how Anna's friend had greeted her. However, in a more formal situation, she might have asked, "And how did you respond?"

The level of formality also is influenced by the personality and style of each individual, and in the United States a rather wide range of styles is accepted. You may, for example, find some instructors and supervisors who adopt a formal style even when talking to you in an informal situation. And, in contrast, others may seem very informal on occasions that are normally formal, especially when compared to people in similar positions in other countries. If you find the variety of styles confusing, you can play it safe by being formal rather than informal. In your conference with an instructor or supervisor, for example, you will no doubt make a good impression if you begin with "good morning" or "good afternoon." Don't be surprised, though, if the person responds with a friendly "hi."

In a formal situation you should not try out any new vocabulary unless you have first checked on the meaning with a reliable source. Finally, speaking and acting in a courteous way always creates a good impression no matter whom you are addressing.

For Discussion

1. Have you ever heard somebody speak to another person in this country in a way that you thought was too formal? Too informal? What did the person say? What was the setting?

2. What are some examples of occasions in your culture when you use formal language and occasions when you use informal language?

Activity 3: Reporting on Informal Expressions

A. Think of as many examples as you can of informal expressions and their possible equivalents in formal language. The teacher or a student will write them on the blackboard. You can use these expressions to get started:

INFORMAL	FORMAL
No way.	Certainly not.
Hi.	Good morning.
Hey, what's happening?	Hello, how are you?

B. For discussion during the next class period, write down an expression that you have heard recently whose level of formality you are not sure about. Make note of the following:

- the speaker and the listener(s)
- the relationship of the speaker to the listener(s)
- the setting
- the topic
- the occasion

Developing Interviewing Skills

When you decide to conduct an interview, you usually have a specific topic in mind, so you select someone who is likely to be a good source for the information you are seeking. You will also have in mind certain points about your topic that you want to find out and, therefore, will need to prepare appropriate questions ahead of time. These questions can be either open-ended or closed. Open-ended questions allow the person being interviewed more freedom in answering and may include feelings and evaluation; closed questions call for more direct, specific responses. Since your goal at the beginning of an interview should be to make the person you are interviewing feel relaxed and comfortable so that the person will talk freely to you, it is better to begin with one or two open-ended questions after some conversational small talk.

EXAMPLE:

You have been assigned to interview a classmate about engagement customs.

OPEN-ENDED QUESTIONS:	Can you tell me about some traditional engagement customs in your country?
	Which of these customs are still popular today?

CLOSED QUESTION:	At what ages do most couples become engaged?

Besides these open-ended and closed questions, you will need to ask many additional questions that you have not prepared ahead of time. These questions will enable you to get more information or clarification about anything the person you are interviewing says that you are not sure about. In addition, during the course of your interview you may need to use a variety of techniques to elicit information, including giving encouragement and showing empathy, asking for repetition or clarification, restating, and interrupting.

Getting additional information　Even when you have specific questions, you will frequently need to ask for more information on a particular point. Here are some expressions you can use to elicit more information:

Q:　What are some engagement customs in your country?

A:　Well, in my country, parents arrange engagements.

Q:
> Could you be more specific?
>
> Could you give me an example?
>
> Could you explain what you mean?
>
> Could you explain what you mean by "arrange"?
>
> Could you add to that?
>
> I wonder if you could tell me more about how it's done.

A:　Well, the parents look for a good partner for their child. They consider the other person's education, social position, and finances. Sometimes religion enters in. Usually relatives and friends help out, but in some cases the parents go through a special person who arranges matches.

Note that the expressions used to elicit more information are polite ones (indicated by the use of "could" and "I wonder if you could"). Note also that the questions are slightly different in content. What kinds of information do they ask for?

Giving encouragement and showing empathy　As you listen to the person you are interviewing, you should show that you are paying attention to the answers and ideas by giving various kinds of verbal and nonverbal feedback. For example, you can make appropriate facial expressions and look directly at the person's face (maintain eye contact). You can nod your head. You can also use short verbal expressions of encouragement. The most common expressions for this purpose are "uh-huh" and "um-hmm," as well as "okay," "yeah," "right," and "yes." These expressions are used while the other person is talking without interrupting him or her, and they serve to encourage the speaker to continue. If there is no feedback of this sort, verbal or nonverbal, the speaker is likely to think that the interviewer is not paying attention or is not interested.

Asking for repetition or clarification   Sometimes in conducting an interview you may not understand (or hear) part or all of what the person says. Here are some ways to ask for repetition or clarification:

A: In some cases parents go through a special person who arranges matches.

Q:
> Pardon me?
>
> I beg your pardon?
>
> Could you say that again, please?
>
> Would you mind repeating that?
>
> Sorry, I don't follow you.
>
> Sorry, I didn't get that.
>
> I'm not sure I understand you.

A: I said that sometimes parents go through a special person who arranges matches.

Q: Oh, that's interesting. Could you explain how that works?

As with the questions seeking more information, note that the expressions for requesting repetition or clarification are formal and thus polite. When interviewing someone, it is not appropriate to use very informal requests for repetition and clarification, such as "Huh?" or "What?" These may be interpreted as impolite.

Restating   If you are not 100 percent sure that you have understood what the speaker has said, a useful approach is to restate or repeat part or all of the speaker's words. If you "check it out" (that is, check your comprehension) in this way, the speaker will often expand on the idea. Here are some ways to restate:

A: Sometimes parents go through a special person who arranges matches.

Q:
> You say they use a special person to arrange a match?
>
> You say there is a special person who arranges matches?
>
> You mean they pay money to someone to find a partner for their son or daughter?

A: Right. Sometimes it is a lot more efficient than relying on family and friends. And it really isn't so expensive when you consider how important it is to find the right partner.

Interrupting   Generally, interrupting a speaker is not considered polite behavior. However, in an interview, interrupting is permissible in some cases. For example, if you do not understand a word or a sentence, it is better to interrupt than to let the speaker talk on at length and then have to repeat or explain something again. Also, you may want to interrupt politely if the person is not answering the question or is changing the subject. Another case in which interrupting is permitted might be termed "technical difficulties." For example, if your pen runs out of ink or your tape recorder runs out of tape, you would want to stop the speaker. Here are some ways to interrupt:

A: Sometimes parents go through a special person who arranges matches.

Q: Oh, that's interesting. Could you explain how that works?

A: Sure. Well, let's say you have a daughter. She's young and attractive but she has only a secondary certificate and you want to find her a well-educated husband so you . . .

Q: Pardon me, but would you repeat that?

Excuse me for interrupting, but what is a secondary certificate?

Sorry for interrupting, but I didn't catch that about the daughter.

Excuse me, but could you wait just a minute? My pencil just broke. . . . Okay, now, you were saying . . .

Also, one of the "rules" of English conversation permits only a few words of overlapping speech, that is, two people talking at the same time. This means that if you are interrupted, you should stop talking almost immediately.

Activity 4:   Practicing Interactive Listening

The class should divide into groups of three persons playing the roles of speaker, listener, and observer. The speaker faces the listener and, for one or two minutes, talks about a recent experience or an assigned topic. The listener should ask for additional information or clarification, restate, and interrupt as necessary in order to properly understand the experience of the speaker. The listener then retells what the speaker said as thoroughly and accurately as possible. Then the observer gives feedback on how well the listener was able to recall what was said, get additional information and clarification, and so on. The group members then change roles. Each group member should have the opportunity to play each role.

ASSIGNMENT: INTERVIEWING A CLASSMATE AND REPORTING ON YOUR INTERVIEW

This assignment involves conducting an interview with a classmate for approximately twenty minutes and reporting on your interview during a subsequent class period. Each partner acts as both interviewer and interviewee. For this assignment you need to do the following:

1. Agree on a topic that you can interview your partner about.
2. Prepare suitable questions on the topic selected.
3. Conduct your interview.
4. Prepare an oral report of your interview.

Preparing Questions for Your Interview

Normally, the interviewer selects the topic of the interview, but in this instance you may consult with your partner about an appropriate topic. Spend five minutes discussing the topic of your partner's choice and another five minutes discussing the topic of your choice. Before the next class period, prepare one or two questions to find out about your partner's background, as well as some open-ended and closed questions on the topic you have agreed on with your partner.

Let us assume, as an example, that your classmate is from Vietnam, and she has decided that the specific topic she would like to be interviewed about is the time she spent in a refugee camp in Thailand before coming to the United States. You think this is an interesting topic and prepare some open-ended and closed questions:

What was it like to be in a refugee camp?

Did you have any good experiences there?

Were you free to leave the camp?

For a successful interview, you and your partner need to develop a good rapport.

How long were you there?

What was the worst thing about being in the camp?

Conducting Your Interview

As you listen to your classmate, make sure that he or she is focusing on one main topic. Pay special attention to details that will make for an interesting report. If you think you will have difficulty reporting on something your partner says, ask for clarification. You should be especially sensitive to emotions shown by your partner and try to be encouraging and supportive. If you are not sure whether your partner would want something reported to others, be sure to ask if it is all right to include it in your report.

Some general guidelines for conducting your interview are as follows:

1. Be prepared to take notes so that you can report on your interview.

2. Throughout the interview, try to use the techniques discussed in this section for getting more information, giving encouragement, asking for repetition and clarification, restating, and interrupting.

3. Greet your partner in a friendly way, doing your best to develop a good rapport.

4. After a sentence or two of small talk, begin by asking your classmate for some background information, for example, full name, country of origin, length of time in the United States, and so on.

5. Continue with an open-ended question on the previously selected specific topic to try to encourage your partner to talk freely.

6. Move on to more specific questions if necessary.

7. Leave the more difficult questions until you feel you have gained your partner's confidence. This means you might want to wait until close to the end of the interview to ask more sensitive questions. Or you might omit them if it seems they would make the person uncomfortable.

8. Finally, be sure to thank the person for the interview.

Some general guidelines for being interviewed are as follows:

1. Respond to questions in a friendly way.

2. Make some eye contact.

3. Answer with information that is relevant to the question. Try not to make your answers too long.

4. If you wish to add some information that is not directly related to the question asked, explain that you are doing so.

5. If you are asked a question that you would feel uncomfortable answering, courteously tell your partner that you would prefer not to answer that question.

ASSIGNMENT: CONSULTING AN INSTRUCTOR OR A SUPERVISOR AND REPORTING ON YOUR CONFERENCE

This assignment involves arranging for a conference with a teacher or supervisor in order to obtain some specific information and writing up a report of

A successful conference with an instructor or supervisor depends on careful preparation and good listening skills.

your conference. In order to have a satisfactory conference, you first need to provide a good reason for requesting the conference. During the conference, you should try to keep your language on a more formal level than you did with your classmate. Of course, it is not necessary to provide support or encouragement in this situation. You should pay special attention to being polite; however, you should also feel free to ask for repetition or clarification of anything you don't understand. For this assignment you need to do the following:

1. Think of something you need some information about for a class or your job.

2. Make an appointment for a conference with an instructor or supervisor.

3. During the conference courteously obtain the information you need.

4. Write a report of your conference (approximately two pages double-spaced).

Preparing Questions for Your Conference

After deciding on a topic for your conference with your instructor or supervisor, you need to prepare some suitable questions just as you did for the interview with your classmate. Let's assume, for example, that a student named Carlos gets a job in an accounting company. During his interview for the job, the personnel officer tells Carlos about probationary periods, performance evaluations, and promotion opportunities, but he is very nervous at that time and does not remember all the details. Therefore, he decides to ask the supervisor for more information. Following are some of the questions he prepares for the conference with his supervisor:

> Could you please tell me about the probationary period?
>
> How will I be evaluated during the probationary period?
>
> How long is the probationary period?
>
> Who will be the main person responsible for evaluating my performance during that period?
>
> Will I be eligible for promotion at the end of that period?
>
> What will happen if my work is not considered satisfactory?

When you have decided on your topic and prepared your questions, you may phone or talk to your supervisor to set up an appointment; for an instructor, it is best to phone during scheduled office hours.

Participating in Your Conference

Here are some guidelines for your conference:

1. Arrive on time. If you arrive early, you must be prepared to wait until the person is ready to see you. If you arrive late, you will make a bad impression.

2. Knock on the door and enter when invited to do so.

3. Greet the person and identify yourself (for example, "Good morning, Ms. Brown. I'm Carlos, the new employee in the accounting department"). Respond politely to whatever the person says; some small talk may occur before you get to the topic of discussion.

4. In general, do not sit down until invited to do so. In the case of an appointment with an instructor, however, it is all right to sit down without waiting to be asked.

5. Once you are seated, explain the reason for your visit as soon as possible. Since you have made the appointment, the responsibility for conducting the discussion is yours, not that of the person you have come to see.

6. During the discussion, try to speak clearly and establish eye contact. In the United States, a quiet voice may indicate low self-confidence, and a lack of eye contact may suggest disrespect.

REPORTING ON YOUR INTERVIEW AND YOUR CONFERENCE

In preparing the oral report on your interview and the written report on your conference, you need to develop paraphrasing skills and distinguish between conventions of spoken and written English.

Paraphrasing

Since you were, of course, not able to take down word for word what was said in your interview or conference, you will need to paraphrase in your reports. To **paraphrase** is to restate the speaker's ideas *in your own words* while retaining the original meaning. Sometimes it is difficult to paraphrase the content of an interview smoothly because of the tendency to repeat the phrase "he (or she) said (or told me)." Clearly, almost everything you report is something the person you were speaking to "said," so it is not necessary to keep repeating such phrases. When you do need to use a reporting word, the ones in the following list provide some alternatives.

NEUTRAL	PERSONAL BELIEF	ADDED INFORMATION
explain	think	repeat
mention	feel	add
observe	believe	go on to say
remark	insist	continue
indicate	claim	
point out	maintain	
	argue	

You can also use phrases such as "according to" and "in the opinion of." When you use these phrases, do *not* also include "he (or she) said."

INCORRECT: According to Anna, she said that people who live here for a while start to adopt the American lifestyle themselves.

CORRECT: According to Anna, people who live here for a while start to adopt the American lifestyle themselves.

One thing you need to be especially careful about when paraphrasing is not to insert your own ideas. Note the following example of the previous statement paraphrased in two different ways.

ORIGINAL: You see, after people live here for a while, they start to adopt the American lifestyle themselves.

POOR PARAPHRASE: According to Anna, people turn into Americans once they come here.

BETTER PARAPHRASE: According to Anna, people begin to follow American customs after they have been in the country for a period of time.

Activity 5:   Practicing Paraphrasing

Paraphrase the following sentences from Rita's interview with Anna.

  a. ANNA: Anyway, I had this friend from Taiwan, who had moved to an area just outside New York, so I thought I'd look her up.

  b. ANNA: I'm not really sure. But it wouldn't hurt to learn as much as possible about the lifestyle in the U.S. before they come here.

Spoken versus Written English

It is very important that the language you use in oral presentations be easily understood by your audience. First of all, let's consider the difference between reading and listening. When you are reading, you can read as rapidly or as slowly as you wish; when you are listening, you have no control over the rate at which you are exposed to the language. In addition, if you don't understand something when you are reading, you can go back and reread the confusing parts. When listening, you do not have a chance to "rehear." Therefore, when speaking, you might need to slow down to assist your audience in understanding.

Another important factor in being understood is language use. Many speakers make the mistake of thinking that the language they use for written reports and essays is equally appropriate for oral presentations. With this in mind, let's talk briefly about the differences in language use in an oral versus a written report. To highlight some of these differences, consider these examples of possible spoken and written conclusions to Rita's report of her interview with Anna.

> **SPOKEN:**   By way of conclusion, I would like to say that I really had a good time interviewing Anna, and I was very interested to hear about her experience with her friend when she first came to the U.S. It was certainly a hard way for her to learn about a cultural difference. I know that you're going to enjoy talking to her too. I'm also looking forward to getting to know the rest of you better.

> **WRITTEN:**   Finally, I very much enjoyed interviewing Anna and hearing about one of her first experiences in coming to terms with the culture of the United States. I hope that, in the future, I will have similar opportunities to meet other classmates and also to learn about their experiences.

Although your audience may be the same for your speech and for your written report—that is, your instructor and your classmates—you are expected to approach them differently in each case. In your speeches you should try to address your audience very directly so that you can establish rapport with them (for example, by using the pronoun *you* wherever appropriate). In contrast, when you write an academic paper, you do not normally address your reader directly by using the pronoun *you;* rather, you put down your ideas without making any direct connection between yourself and the reader. Notice in the previous example how Rita addresses her classmates *directly* but writes *about* her classmates.

Now let's consider another difference between the spoken and written versions. Often, the spoken version is longer; a speaker usually needs to say a little more to get the message across to an audience than is necessary when writing. As a result, in a speech the sentence structure is usually simpler, with frequent use of common connectors like *and, but, so, then, when,* and *because.* By using this type of sentence structure, you will help your listeners follow what you are saying. In writing, however, sentences tend to be more tightly structured, with the various parts of the sentence more closely inter-woven. After all, as a reader, you can always go back and read more complex sentences over if you don't grasp the meaning the first time. In the previous example the first sentence of the spoken conclusion uses the simple connectors "and" and "when," while the written conclusion uses the phrase "in coming to terms with."

Since you will be speaking to a group of non-native speakers, the vo-cabulary you choose should be familiar, frequently used words. Also, you can use more informal English in your oral report than you will in your written report.

> **SPOKEN:**   I <u>really had a good time</u> interviewing Anna . . .
>
> **WRITTEN:**   I <u>very much enjoyed</u> interviewing Anna . . .

Yet another difference between a spoken and a written report is in the way each introduces direct quotations. When speaking you have to indicate that you are going to quote someone by using the phrase "and I quote." Some-times speakers also use hand gestures to indicate the beginning and end of a quotation. In contrast, when writing you use a reporting verb and then simply enclose what is said in quotation marks, which indicate to the reader that you are using the exact words of a writer or speaker.

> **SPOKEN:**   Anna admitted, and I quote—it's just natural to start to follow the ways of the culture you live in—end quote.
>
> **WRITTEN:**   Anna admitted, "It's just natural to start to follow the ways of the culture you live in."

A final difference is that you can see how a written report is laid out, but you can't see the structure of an oral report. Although both a speech and a paper normally have an introduction, a body, and a conclusion, these parts are usually more obvious in a paper because of the physical layout. It is, there-fore, very important in a speech that you emphasize your main points and use clear transitions when you move from one point to another. In the speech you give for this assignment, the main transitions you make will be (1) between your introductory background information and the main idea discussed in your interview or conference and (2) between the end of the body of your speech and the conclusion. Although there should be clear transitions in both the written and spoken reports, they should be more noticeable in the speech. In an oral report you need to use appropriate words to make transitions; you also mark them by pausing and changing the tone of your voice. In the previ-ous example the spoken conclusion uses the words "by way of conclusion" as a transition while the written version uses the less obvious word "finally." Here is an example of the kind of transition you might make for each version at the end of the introduction:

SPOKEN: Good morning, everyone. Like all of you, I enjoyed interviewing one of our classmates during a class period last week. The person I interviewed was Anna Ng—some of you know her already, and the rest will get to know her soon. Anna comes from Taiwan, and she's been here about two years. We had agreed ahead of time that I would interview her about a difficult cultural experience she had when she first came to the U.S.

Now to start off with, let me give you some background to the experience. When Anna left Taiwan, she went first to New York City to study at the City University there. . . .

WRITTEN: Last week I had the pleasure of interviewing one of my classmates, Anna Ng. Anna comes from Taiwan and has been living in the United States for about two years. In a previous discussion, we had decided that the main topic of our interview would be an experience Anna had that reflected a difference between the culture in Taiwan and the culture in the United States.

Anna's experience began soon after she arrived in New York, where she went to study at the City University of New York. . . .

For Discussion

1. Have you ever had a comment written on your essay asking you not to use the pronoun *you*? When did this happen?

2. Can you think of a lecture or a speech that you found difficult to understand? What do you think was the main reason for your difficulty?

Preparing the Oral Report on Your Interview

Rita's introduction and conclusion in the section on spoken versus written English illustrate two parts of both spoken and written reports. The third component, the body, should focus on the main topic of your interview.

In the body you need to include enough information to make your topic clear to your listeners and readers. However, you do not need to include *everything* that was mentioned; for instance, it would not be necessary for Rita to include in her report the details about Anna buying the map and riding the subway.

When preparing your oral report, remember that it is not a good idea to read or to memorize your speech. You can use note cards to remind yourself of the points you want to make. Here are the notes that Rita took during the first part of her interview:

> Interview – 2/12/91
> Anna Ng
> Comes from Taiwan
> Been here 2 years
> Had problem –
>   1st came here
> (Difficult cultural exper.)

When Rita prepares the note cards for her oral report using this information, her first note card looks like this:

> 1.
>
> Enjoyed interv – last week
> Anna Ng – some know her
> Taiwan – U.S. abt. 2 yrs
> Intrv – diff. cult exper.

On this card, Rita includes a note that she enjoyed the interview to introduce her oral report and bring in her partner's name. She then condenses the rest of the information in her written notes so that it will fit on the note card. At the same time, she makes sure that she has written enough information on the card to remind herself of what she wants to say.

Activity 6:   *Speaking from a Note Card*

Watch as your instructor gives the introduction to Rita's oral report using the first note card, and count the number of times that he or she looks at the card while speaking. Now, with a partner, take turns giving the same introduction until you can do so smoothly. Practice alternately looking at the note card and at your partner. Try to look at the card only three or four times.

Activity 7:   *Preparing and Speaking from a Note Card*

A.   Use the following notes from Rita's interview of Anna to prepare a note card for the next part of Rita's report.

> From Taiwan
> Went 1st to N.Y.C.
> Studied at C.U.N.Y. —
>   one semester
> Had friend fr. Taiwan
> Friend lived outside N.Y.C.
> Decided to visit her

B.   Form small groups. Each group member should practice speaking to the group using the note card prepared for part A. Practice alternately looking at the note card and at your group members. Try to look at the card only three or four times.

Activity 8:   Comparing Notes and Paragraphs

In the instructions for the conference assignment, you read the questions that Carlos prepared for a conference with his supervisor. An excerpt from the conference follows. Prepare (1) an oral report on note cards and (2) a one-paragraph written report to introduce and summarize the following part of Carlos's conference. Your first note card and the first sentence of your paragraph should indicate that Carlos is a new employee in an accounting firm and that he had a conference with his supervisor, Ms. Brown. Be prepared to present your oral report in class and to discuss the differences between the oral and written versions.

CARLOS: Well, first, could you please tell me about the probationary period?

MS. BROWN: Yes. All employees are on probation when they are first hired. During that period their work is evaluated. And they are not considered permanent until they have completed the probationary period with a satisfactory work record.

CARLOS: And how will I be evaluated during the probationary period?

MS. BROWN: In several different ways. One of the most important things we will look at will be the accuracy and efficiency of your work; another will be your ability to learn new tasks reasonably quickly; and we'll also consider your attitude toward your work and the way you get along with your co-workers.

CARLOS: How long is the probationary period?

MS. BROWN: Six months.

CARLOS: Well, it sounds as if almost everything I do is going to be evaluated. But I'll certainly do my best to measure up!

Activity 9: Preparing a Spoken and a Written Advertisement

Choose a product you would like to advertise, and then do the following:

1. Prepare note cards to give a short speech advertising the product.

2. Write a short paragraph describing the good points of the product.

3. Be prepared to present your oral summary in class and to discuss the differences between your oral and written summaries.

Preparing the Written Report on Your Conference

Your written report on the conference with your instructor or supervisor may include the following:

- an introduction in which you give (1) the name and position of the person with whom you had the conference and (2) the subject of the conference

- a report of the information you obtained

- a conclusion in which you explain how you will benefit from obtaining this information

Practicing Your Oral Report

First, review the criteria on the evaluation form at the end of this unit. Pay attention to these features of content and delivery as you practice. If possible, audiotape yourself as you practice delivering your speech in front of a mirror. We suggest going through the following steps:

1. Start the tape and take note of the time.

2. As you go through your speech, check your posture, facial expressions, and gestures.

3. Check your finishing time.

4. Play back the tape and check your fluency, rate, and pronunciation. Check whether you spoke as clearly as possible.

5. Delete or add information according to whether your speech took more or less than the allotted time.

Note cards can help you keep eye contact with your audience while reminding you of the points you want to make.

6. Practice several more times, each time concentrating on one or two areas that need correction.

7. If possible, practice again in front of a native speaker of English and try to follow up on any helpful suggestions the listener makes.

Listening and Evaluating

As your classmates give their reports, you will need to listen actively, keeping in mind the criteria on the evaluation form that follows. First, pay attention to the background information that may be helpful to you when working with the student later. Then listen for the main topic of the interview and the details the speaker provides about the topic to make it interesting. Finally, notice how the speaker concludes the report. As you write an evaluation, try to offer some positive comments before making suggestions about improvements needed for the next presentation.

Unit 2   Report on Interview

Speaker _____   RATING SYSTEM: $+$ = excellent

Evaluator _____ _____ $\sqrt{}$ = average

                                                                                     $-$ = weak

Content   **Delivery**

_____ Introduction (background information)   _____ Volume

_____ Focus on one main topic   _____ Rate

        Topic _____   _____ Comprehensibility

_____ Supporting details   _____ Posture

_____ Conclusion   _____ Eye contact

Comments and suggestions for next presentation:

Unit 3

Providing Information:
Instructions and Demonstrations

SAMPLE SPEECH

As you read or listen to the following transcribed speech, make note of what you must do to be prepared for an earthquake.

The brief outline that follows was shown on an overhead projector. The speaker's references to the points on this outline are indicated in the speech by brackets.

BEFORE AN EARTHQUAKE	DURING AN EARTHQUAKE	AFTER AN EARTHQUAKE
Meeting place	Home or office	Car
Contact person	Public building	Phone
Furniture	High-rise building	Injured people
Utilities	Outdoors	Public building
Supplies	Car	Home—utilities
		Radio

ARE YOU PREPARED FOR AN EARTHQUAKE?

Good morning! I wonder if any of you were anywhere near San Francisco on the afternoon of October 17, 1989. I'm sure I won't have to remind any of you who were in that area what happened then; I bet you could even tell me exactly what you were doing at 5:04 that evening.

Why? (*pause*) Right, that was when the earthquake struck.

Now maybe you think that you don't have to worry about earthquakes—they never happen where you live.

That's just what I used to think about Great Britain, where I was raised. But it has recently experienced several earthquakes.

And devastating earthquakes have occurred in the Philippines, China, Central America, the Middle East, and the Soviet Union, all within the past decade.

In the United States, the states most likely to have earthquakes are Alaska, California, and Hawaii. However, other states have also experienced earthquakes and will probably have them again.

So, no matter where you live, it would be a good idea for you to make a few simple preparations and to find out what to do during and after an earthquake.

There are a number of things you can do before an earthquake occurs to help you cope with the situation when it happens. [Before an earthquake]

Put yourself in this situation. An earthquake has just occurred and you're alive and well. What do you think your first worry would be?

The safety of your family members, of course! You should plan to meet at a place where you can all get together if you can't get to your home. [Meeting place]

Another thing you could do is choose a relative or friend who lives in a different state as a contact person. [Contact person] After an earthquake the family members can call this person to find out where the others are and how they are doing.

Now that you have a plan for your family members, you need to take a look around your home and make sure that you have a safe environment.

As I prepared this speech, I couldn't help noticing the shelves crammed with books over my desk. I wondered how I would feel if they all fell on top of me! I think I should have the shelves moved.

You should try to secure as much heavy furniture as you can, including wall units that contain all your valuable stereo equipment. Also check how secure mirrors and pictures are. Especially if they are hanging over your bed! [Furniture]

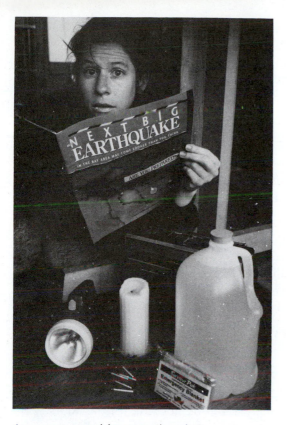

Are you prepared for an earthquake?

Besides making objects secure—oh, I forgot to mention your water heater among the things that need to be secured—you should learn how to shut off the water, gas, and electricity in case the supply lines are broken. [Utilities]

Another thing you have to think about is having on hand those items or supplies that will be extremely helpful to you when there's a serious earthquake. [Supplies]

First—what's this? (*Holds up a flashlight*) Right, a flashlight. It's essential to find things and see your way around when you have no electricity.

Here is something else you should have. (*Holds up a radio*) A battery-operated radio. And don't forget some spare batteries—because you know they always seem to go dead when you need them to work.

Our family had absolutely no idea how serious the San Francisco earthquake was until we listened to the radio. We also learned on the radio where we could go for emergency shelter if we could no longer stay in our home and which businesses and schools would be closed the next day.

Other useful items to have on hand are a fire extinguisher, a portable stove, and a first aid kit in case anyone is hurt.

Of course, you don't want to go hungry or thirsty, so you should keep a supply of canned and dried foods, and a supply of bottled water for everyone in your family.

Needless to say, all these items should be stored in a place where they are easy to get.

Now that you have made all these necessary preparations, what should you do when you feel the earth starting to quake? [During an earthquake]

Well, experts advise that if you are in your home or office, you should get under a table or a desk or stand in a doorway. This will protect you from anything falling from above. [Home or office]

If you are in a crowded public place like a department store, try to move away from display shelves. But do not rush for the doors. You can be injured by getting caught up in a crowd of panicky people. [Public place]

If you work in a high-rise building, you should keep away from the windows and the outside walls of the building. [High-rise building]

If you're outdoors, you need to move as far away from trees, buildings, walls, and power lines as possible. [Outdoors]

And if you are driving your car, pull over to the side of the road and stay inside until the shaking stops. [Car]

Now that I have told you how to make preparations for an earthquake and what to do during an earthquake, I will continue with some advice about what you can do after the earth stops quaking. [After an earthquake]

If you are in your car, you may be able to drive home if your car is okay and the roads are passable. But, you will need to be prepared for traffic lights that are not working and other traffic problems too. [Car] But, if you are at home, you should not plan on driving anywhere. You need to leave the streets clear for emergency vehicles!

And you should wait to call your contact person for a couple of hours since phone lines are also needed for emergencies. [Phone]

Of course, wherever you are, if you are with other people, the first thing you should do is to help anyone who is injured and apply first aid if practicable. [Injured people] Don't try to move people who are seriously injured unless they are in immediate danger.

If you are in a public building, you should exit as soon as you can do so safely. Use the stairs and not the elevators. [Public building]

You must also leave your home if there is danger of any part of it collapsing; otherwise, you should check for breaks in any of the utility lines and turn the utilities off if necessary. [Home—utilities]

Once you have taken care of all these urgent matters, then you can turn on your portable radio and listen for instructions and news reports. [Radio]

To sum up, my advice to you is to make the simple preparations I have suggested and be sure you know what to do during and after an earthquake.

You may end up with no running water, no gas, no electricity; your phone line may be down. And emergency services will be assigned to areas that have the most serious damage. So help could be a long time in coming.

That is exactly what happened after the earthquake in San Francisco. Emergency services were concentrated in the Marina district, which experienced the heaviest damage. In the meantime, other districts had to go without gas and electricity for several days before the utility company was able to restore these services.

My son was one of those who had this experience. It took four days before the electricity was restored to his apartment.

Clearly, then, the more you are able to rely on your own resources when a major earthquake occurs, the better the chances are for you and your family to survive!

Remember the well-known words of the boy scout motto— "Be prepared!"

For Discussion

1. How does the speaker attract the listeners' interest at the beginning of the speech?

2. Does the speaker have an organizational plan for the speech? What is it?

3. What words or phrases does the speaker use to make transitions from one point to the next?

4. Where in the speech does the speaker try to make the speech seem personal to the audience and thus create rapport?

5. How does the speaker structure the conclusion?

6. What visual aids does the speaker use?

DEMONSTRATING PROCESSES OR PROVIDING INSTRUCTIONS

Information speeches serve a wide range of purposes, but they are all intended to provide the audience with greater knowledge and clearer understanding of a particular topic. You have already presented reports on information you gathered in class surveys and in interviews with classmates. In this unit the purpose of your information speeches will be to demonstrate processes or provide instructions. Such presentations are very common in today's world. For example, as an office manager, you may have to explain some new procedures to other employees in the office, or as a leader you may have to show a group of volunteers how to perform a particular task. The speech that opens this unit might have been given by a concerned individual as a service to members of his own local community group. Because it is likely that you will participate in similar activities in the future, knowing how to prepare and give such a speech should prove useful to you.

ASSIGNMENT: GIVING AN INSTRUCTIVE OR DEMONSTRATION SPEECH

The main assignment for this unit is a four- to five-minute speech in which you instruct the members of the class about *how to do* something. Keep the following guidelines for your speech in mind:

1. Clearly demonstrate a process or provide instructions.

2. Use some kind of visual aid or include a demonstration. (You may use *willing* members of the class as helpers.)

3. Include an introduction and a conclusion planned according to the guidelines given in this unit.

4. Speak from an outline or note cards.

FINDING A TOPIC

As you begin work on this assignment, you'll need to first analyze your audience so that you can choose a suitable topic. Then you will need to narrow the topic to fit the assignment.

Analyzing Your Audience

If you are asked by a group of people to give a speech on a specific topic, you can normally assume that your audience already has an interest in what you have to say and that they recognize you as a person having special knowledge of, or expertise about, the topic. However, you will probably still need to do some research into the background and interests of your audience.

Let us consider the case of a speaker representing a university that has taken over a building with the intention of using it for a medical research facility. A university representative has been asked to give speeches about the new facility to three different groups of people: students and science teachers from a nearby high school, some employees who might be transferred to the facility, and property owners from the neighborhood in which the facility is located. Would it be advisable to give the same speech to all three groups? Clearly, it would not be. The teachers and students would be interested in how visits to and possibly internships in the facility could be coordinated with science classes at the school. The employees might want to know what condition the building is in, which of them are likely to be transferred to the new site, and how the research is going to be divided between the new site and the old site. The property owners, of course, would be interested in any environmental concerns that might affect the value of their property and in whether the site would have its own parking area. To address these audiences effectively, the university representative would have to keep the different interests of the three groups uppermost in mind when preparing the speeches. Indeed, no effective speaker ever disregards the interests and concerns of the audience.

In your case, your audience will be your classmates. Therefore, you should keep in mind their backgrounds when selecting topics for your speeches.

Choosing Your Topic

The following guidelines should help you find an appropriate speech topic.

1. **Choose a topic that interests your audience.** Clearly, your classmates have not come to hear a speech on a specific topic, so you will have to be prepared to put in a little extra effort to arouse and maintain their interest. All audiences become more involved when listening to a speech on a topic that they can relate to. Since this speech assignment calls for instructions or a demonstration, try to come up with something that would be useful and/or enjoyable for your classmates to learn.

2. **Choose a topic that takes account of your audience's background knowledge.** A speech on nuclear fusion is fine if you are speaking to a group of nuclear physicists, but a general audience won't have enough background knowledge to follow what you are saying and will probably be confused and bored. Should you choose to give a speech on a highly technical topic to a general audience like your classmates, you will need to express yourself in simple, nontechnical language and offer a full explanation of unfamiliar terms.

    Don't choose a topic that everyone in your audience already knows about. For instance, if you are speaking to a group of Chinese, it would be ridiculous to talk about how to use chopsticks. If you choose to speak on a common topic, try to find some new way of presenting it (for example, how to teach foreigners to use chopsticks). In any case, your choice of topic should show respect for your audience's knowledge and abilities.

3. **Choose a topic that interests you.** If a topic really interests you, there is a good chance that it will interest your audience, too. You must be able to show a genuine enthusiasm about your topic in order to make your audience equally enthusiastic. If you are not excited about your topic, you can be sure your audience won't be either.

4. **Choose a topic that fits the time assigned for the speech.** Because you will want to make several main points about your topic, as well as provide supporting details for each of these points, choose a topic that can be adequately covered within the time allowed for your speech.

How are you going to find a topic that conforms to these guidelines? The best way is to start with yourself. Think about your hobbies, your interests, and your experience, and consider whether any of these could be a source of interesting information that you could share with your audience. Another good source of ideas is magazines and newspapers. What sections do you always turn to? Food? Sports?

In any case, although you may look for ideas in a variety of places, the topic that you finally decide on should be one that you are already knowledgeable about. If you learn to prepare a special dish just for your speech, there is every possibility that something will go wrong during the demonstration due either to your unfamiliarity with what you are doing or to your nervousness while giving the speech, or possibly both. Also, if you do not have experience in what you are demonstrating, you will be unable to answer questions with any authority.

Here is a list of possible topics to help you get started:

ENVIRONMENT

gardening techniques

potting plants

preparing materials for recycling

saving water

taking precautions against toxics

GROOMING

dressing for success

wearing accessories

caring for hair

giving a haircut/perm

LIFE SKILLS

changing oil in a car

jump-starting a car

preparing for exams

making investments

securing a loan

setting up a budget

writing a résumé

HOBBIES

aspects of art

aspects of photography

doing a magic trick

making a jewelry item

making a kite

learning the rumba
(tango, samba)

palm reading

playing a game

sumi painting

tracing your family tree

SOCIAL AND CULTURAL EVENTS

arranging flowers

giving a successful party

making a greeting card

preparing one aspect of a wedding ceremony

HEALTH AND EXERCISE	SPORTS
CPR	aspects of sports (improving your tennis serve)
first aid	
losing weight	backpacking
preventing a common injury	jogging
planning a nutritious diet	rafting
relieving stress	running
martial arts exercises	skiing
relaxation exercises	swimming
warm-up and cool-down exercises	

Narrowing Down Your Topic

It is the details that give color and liveliness to your speech, so after you have come up with a general idea, you need to work on narrowing your topic so that you can cover the main ideas and include interesting details within the time limit for your speech. You need to choose one aspect to focus on and develop it with relevant and interesting ideas. A good way to do this is to brainstorm—that is, write down all the ideas you have that are associated with your general idea. Let's suppose you picked "swimming" from the topics list because you enjoy swimming and you think you know more about it than some of the other topics. Here are some ideas that might appear on your brainstorming list:

freestyle	competitive swimming
breast stroke	school teams
butterfly	Olympic teams
backstroke	swimming as exercise
diving	swimming in pools
children's swimming lessons	swimming in the ocean
adult swimming lessons	lifeguarding

Because you teach children swimming during the summer, the idea that stands out for you is children's swimming lessons. You realize that many of your classmates may know how to swim, but you think many of them may not have taught others how to swim. They may have younger brothers and sisters, nieces or nephews, or, someday, children of their own, and it could be useful for them to be able to teach these young children how to swim. You then settle on the topic "An Introductory Swimming Lesson for a Five-Year-Old Child."

Activity 1:   Deciding on Appropriate Topics

For the following two situations, look at the audience description and the assigned time limit. Put a plus sign (+) next to the topics that would be appropriate, and a minus sign (−) next to the topics that would be inappropriate. Be prepared to discuss your answers.

EXAMPLE

Audience: new college students

Time limit: ten minutes

  − how to tell time (too simple for the audience)

  − how to use the library (would take too long)

  + how to use the *Readers' Guide to Periodical Literature*

  + how to use the local bus system

a. Audience: general adults

Time limit: ten minutes

  _____ how to read palms

  _____ how to set a VCR to record a program

  _____ how to play baseball

  _____ how to use a word processor

  _____ how to set up a personal budget

b. Audience: general adults

Time limit: five minutes

  _____ how to do a magic trick

  _____ how to play the guitar

  _____ how to floss and brush your teeth

  _____ how to write a short business letter

  _____ how to repot a plant

Activity 2:   Narrowing Down Topics

First, choose two general subjects that you are interested in and brainstorm on your own until you narrow down the general subjects to two possible topics for each subject. Then form small groups. Group members should assist one another in selecting a topic for the demonstration speech assignment by going over the following questions:

1. Will the topic probably interest a majority of the class members?

2. Does the person show enthusiasm about the topic?

3. Has the general topic been narrowed down enough for the person to be able to provide specific details about the topic?

4. Can the person effectively cover the topic within the time allowed?

ORGANIZING THE BODY OF YOUR SPEECH

Once you have come up with a clearly defined topic, you then have to decide what you are going to say about it. Because your speech has to be completed within a specified time period, there is obviously a limit to how much you can say. You will want to make sure that you cover the main points of your topic; this may mean that you have to discard a lot of material. In addition, you will need to include key subpoints and supporting details. To ensure that you have a sensible organization, you will have to prepare an outline of your speech. Finally, you will want to ensure that you provide effective transitions between the various elements of your speech.

Deciding on Main Points

Deciding on the main points of your speech is the beginning of organization and helps to give you an overall view of your speech. When *you* are clear about your main points, you can usually make them clear to your audience.

How do you come up with these main points? Once again, you can brainstorm for the information you will need to include to make your instructions or demonstration clear. After you have come up with a list of ideas, examine them to see which seem to be main points, and which subpoints. When you have two or more related subpoints, you may be able to think of a heading for a main point to cover these subpoints. Research has shown that five main points are usually the maximum number that an average audience will retain, so keep that in mind. As an example, consider the following list of ideas for a speech on "How to Take a Good Photograph":

buying a camera	shooting the picture
knowing the camera	favorite pictures
locating a subject	pictures of people
judging distance	scenic views
framing a picture	using a flash
the right amount of light	choosing the appropriate lens
the right angle of light	

The task now is to organize the list so that we have not more than five main points. In order to do this, it will be necessary to group several items under a main heading and possibly discard some items. Here is how it might be done.

TOPIC: How to Take a Good Photograph

MAIN POINT 1:   Lighting

the right amount of light
the right angle of light   } subpoints
using a flash

MAIN POINT 2:   Composing the picture

locating a subject
judging distance
framing the picture   } subpoints
pictures of people
scenic views

MAIN POINT 3:   Knowing the camera
choosing the appropriate lens } subpoint

MAIN POINT 4:   Shooting the picture

In this regrouping we end up with four main points and some subpoints. We have dropped "buying a camera" since it seems like too much information to cover in this speech. We have also dropped "favorite pictures" because it doesn't seem to fit well with the other ideas.

The main points of a speech should be equally related to the topic. Do our four main points seem equally related? Even if all the ideas in the list seem to be equally related—that is, nothing in the list seems like a subpoint—it is still better to group the ideas under a few headings.

Having decided on the main points, the next thing to consider is the order in which you will present them. In the brief outline that precedes the speech "Are You Prepared for an Earthquake?" the main points are what to do *before, during,* and *after* an earthquake. The main points for that speech are clearly organized in time order, also known as chronological order. Those of you who choose to demonstrate a single process will want to follow a similar time-related order. For instance, if you give a speech on how to change the oil in a car, you will need to go through the various steps in a certain order, so the order of your main points will already be established for you.

Although the speech "How to Take a Good Photograph" does not have the same built-in steps as a speech on changing oil, we might put our main points in the following order because it seems the most logical to us:

knowing the camera

checking the lighting

composing the picture

shooting the picture

Putting "knowing the camera" first seems logical because without a camera, and without knowing how the camera works, you cannot take a picture. Next, you cannot take a picture without sufficient light, so that makes "checking the lighting" a logical second point. Finally, you need to compose a picture before you shoot it.

If time order or logical order do not work out naturally for your speech, you will need to organize your main points in some other way. One way might be to show something easier before something more difficult; for instance, if you chose to demonstrate different ways to tie a tie, it would make sense to start with the easiest knot.

Another method that speakers use to determine how to order their main points is the order of importance; some speakers put the least important idea first and work up to the most important, while others do the reverse. For example, let's say you were giving a speech to a class of accounting students who were about to graduate and were advising them about points they could stress in their job interviews. You might consider their ability to communicate well with clients to be the most important, or you might think their ability to audit clients' accounts accurately to be the most important. Your opinion would then influence the order in which you put these points.

Planning Subpoints and Supporting Details

Having decided on your main points, your next task is to provide subpoints and supporting details for each of them. You may need or want to consult written sources or interview someone in order to gather necessary information. For example, you might have had some experience as a tutor and so decide to give a speech on "How to Be an Effective Tutor." By talking to other tutors, you could probably get additional subpoints and supporting details.

Certainly your audience's ability to clearly understand your speech will depend on how well you support each of your main points. The subpoints should relate equally to the main point, just as the main points relate equally to the topic.

Outlining

The best way to get a clear picture of your main points and your subpoints is to prepare a rough outline. To begin, jot down your main points, leaving about half a page of space below each; then list what you think should be the subpoints and supporting details under each one. We will demonstrate here with one of our main points, "composing the picture."

COMPOSING THE PICTURE

locate subject—center?

judge distance—simple and other cameras

frame picture

pictures of people

scenic views

As we look over the list, we find that "locate subject," "judge distance," and "frame picture" could serve as good subpoints. However, "pictures of people" and "scenic views" do not seem to fit with them; they certainly don't describe an action as the others do. We decide to make a new subpoint to cover them, "decide what to include." Just as we did with the main points, we then have to decide on a logical order for the subpoints. Here, our subpoints become:

> decide what to include
>
> locate main subject
>
> judge distance
>
> frame picture

The next step is to list some supporting details for each of the subpoints. This time we follow the traditional numbering and lettering system for outlines—that is, roman numerals for main points, uppercase (capital) letters for subpoints, arabic numerals for supporting details, and lowercase letters for further supporting details. As an example, here is how the part of the outline for our third main point, "composing the picture," might be written:

III. Composing the picture
    A. Decide what to include
        1. Decide on person(s)
        2. Select scene
    B. Locate main subject
        1. Do not place in center
        2. Select appropriate focal point
    C. Judge distance
        1. Use eye—simple cameras
        2. Set lens—other cameras
    D. Frame picture
        1. Check edges for anything unwanted
        2. Check edges for anything missing

You may be asking yourself why you have to go to the trouble of making an outline. First, an outline is a visual way of showing the organization of your ideas. It clearly sets out your main points and your subpoints so that you can see how they relate to one another. Second, it is easy to change; you can move the ideas around if you want to try a different order, and you can add additional points or details or take some out if it seems appropriate. Third, an outline can help establish in your mind ahead of time the points that you will

An instructive speech like this one on how to take a good photograph guides the audience through the process step by step.

cover in your speech, thus making you better prepared. Finally, your outline provides a good source for the information that you put on your note cards.

Following is a complete outline of the body of the speech on "How to Take a Good Photograph." The outline also contains notes about the use of visual aids, which will be discussed later in this unit.

   I. Knowing the camera
      A. Read camera manual
         1. Choose appropriate lens
         2. Obtain appropriate film
            a. Read film info
      B. Check automatic or manual settings
      C. Check light meter, shutter speed, depth of field

Figure 3.1   Sample Handout

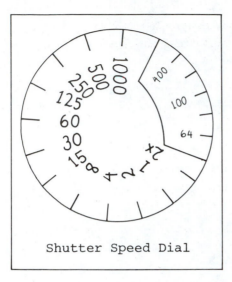

Shutter Speed Dial

II. Checking the lighting
  A. Adjust for amount of light, that is, exposure
    1. Exposure set automatically—automatic cameras
    2. Adjust aperture and set shutter speed—manually operated cameras (refer to visual aid showing shutter speed settings) [see Figure 3.1]
    3. Use flash if not enough light indoors (demonstrate)
  B. Plan for direction of light—45-degree angle from camera (show picture with light striking subject directly and one taken with 45-degree angle)
III. Composing the picture
  A. Decide what to include
    1. Decide on person(s)
    2. Select scene (show large examples of photos of scenes)
  B. Locate main subject
    1. Do not place in center
    2. Select appropriate focal point

    C. Judge distance
       1. Use eye—simple cameras
       2. Set lens—other cameras (demonstrate estimating distance from a person or an object)
    D. Frame picture
       1. Check edges for anything unwanted
       2. Check edges for anything missing
IV. Shooting the picture
    A. Using hand-held camera
       1. Stand, sit, kneel in balanced position
       2. Hold camera against face with both hands (demonstrate with own camera)
       3. Use breathing techniques
       4. Shoot at $1/125$ secs.
    B. Using tripod
       1. Balance tripod
       2. Attach camera securely
       3. Employ cable release to shoot

Activity 3:   *Choosing and Ordering Main Points*

Decide which of the following main points you would use for a speech on flower arranging and which you might discard. Then put them in the order you think would be most appropriate. Be prepared to explain your reasons for selecting this order.

    arranging flowers and foliage

    cost of flowers and foliage

    selecting flowers and foliage

    preparing suitable support materials

    different types of containers

    selecting an appropriate vase

Activity 4:   Choosing and Ordering Main Points and Subpoints

In small groups decide which of the items on the following list would be more suitable for main points and which would be better for subpoints for a speech on "How to Succeed in a New Job." After you have decided on the main points, make an outline, putting the main points and subpoints in the order you consider most logical. Your group should be prepared to provide reasons for selecting items as main points and for putting them in the order chosen.

being friendly

showing initiative

getting work done on time

developing a cooperative attitude toward other employees

making independent suggestions

not complaining about others

being on time

taking a few calculated risks

showing responsibility toward your work

helping others feel good about their jobs

being conscientious about details

accepting help and suggestions gracefully

showing up regularly

being willing to try out new ideas on your own time

Activity 5:   Evaluating the Body of Your Speech and Your Classmates' Speeches

For homework write out an outline for the body of your speech. In class form small groups; exchange outlines and then answer the following questions about each outline.

1. How many main points does the outline show?
2. Do the main points relate equally to the topic?

3. Are the main points in a logical order?

4. Does each main point seem to have sufficient subpoints and supporting details to make it clear?

After answering the questions and discussing the answers, select one member's outline to put on the board for class discussion. Choose an outline you especially like or one you want feedback on.

Making Transitions

It is important to make a noticeable transition between the introduction and the body and between the body and the conclusion of a speech. But these are not the only transitions you will have to use to make your speech clear to your audience. The audience needs to know when you are moving from one main point to another and to understand the relationship among the subpoints. Besides helping the audience keep track of the content of your speech, your transitions should make your speech flow smoothly from one point to the next.

Transitions can take several different forms. Perhaps the most common types for a demonstration speech are *first, second, third*. Such transitions are helpful, as well as being clearer than saying "another" to introduce each new point. If you use this system for your main points, however, you must find another way of indicating your subpoints in order to prevent confusion. Keep in mind, too, that it is best to use only one set of numbers per speech and also not to number beyond five.

If you order your points according to importance, it would be possible to use the transitions *more important* and *most important* to introduce your second and third points. Other words and phrases that you can use to give more information are *in addition, besides, moreover, again, also, then,* and *and*. Remember to vary these transitions; a speaker who repeatedly uses *and then* or *also* to connect ideas will not give a smooth speech and is likely to lose the interest of the audience.

While these single-word or short-phrase transitions are useful for joining subpoints, it is better to use more noticeable transitions to highlight your main points. One way to make transitions between main points is to ask a rhetorical question, that is, a question that you go on to answer yourself. Asking such questions can be a good way of maintaining the audience's attention because they usually think of their own answers while you are speaking and compare them with yours. Another way to make transitions is to refer to the previous point or points you have made before continuing with the next main point. You can do this by using a short phrase or, sometimes, a complete sentence. Here are some examples of transitions that could be used in the speeches "How to Make a Beautiful Flower Arrangement" and "Are You Prepared for an Earthquake?"

SINGLE-WORD AND SHORT-PHRASE TRANSITIONS   (to join subpoints)

<u>Now</u> you are ready to work with the flowers and the foliage. <u>First</u>, trim off the leaves from the bottom of the stems; these leaves just get in the way and make the water dirty. <u>The next thing to do</u> is to stick each flower into the support material in different spots and estimate the height that you want for each flower. A flower arrangement is usually prettier and more interesting when you vary the heights of the flowers. <u>Then</u>, remove each flower one by one and cut it so that it will be the right height. <u>After cutting them</u>, . . .

RHETORICAL QUESTION   (to introduce the next main point)

Of course, you don't want to go hungry or thirsty, so you should keep a supply of canned and dried foods, and a supply of bottled water for everyone in your family. Needless to say, all these items should be stored in a place where they are easy to get.

Now that you have made all these necessary preparations, <u>what should you do when you feel the earth starting to quake?</u>

REFERENCE TO PREVIOUS POINT

Short phrase (to introduce the next subpoint)

You should try to secure as much heavy furniture as you can, including wall units that contain all your valuable stereo equipment. Also check how secure mirrors and pictures are. Especially if they are hanging over your bed!

<u>Besides making objects secure</u> . . . you should learn how to shut off the water, gas, and electricity in case the supply lines are broken.

Complete sentence (to introduce last main point)

<u>Now that I have told you how to make preparations for an earthquake and what to do during an earthquake, I will continue with some advice about what you can do after the earth stops quaking.</u>

Activity 6:   *Practicing Transitions*

A.   Using the outline for the body of "How to Take a Good Photograph," do the following:

1. Make up a rhetorical question to introduce the second or third main point.

2. For main point II, "checking the lighting," use a phrase to summarize subpoint A as you move to subpoint B.

3. In one sentence refer to the second and third main points as you introduce the fourth one.

B.   Prepare note cards for each of these transitions and be prepared to present the part of the speech that incorporates the transition to the class.

Activity 7:   *Planning and Practicing Your Own Transitions*

A.   Using the outline for the body of your own speech, do the following:

1. Make up a transition to connect two of your main points.

2. Make up a transition to connect two of your subpoints.

3. Make up a rhetorical question as a transition at a suitable place in your speech.

B.   Prepare note cards for the parts of your speech that you have made up transitions for. In small groups, deliver those parts of your speech to the other members. The other members of the group should be able to identify your transitions and the points that you are connecting.

PREPARING YOUR CONCLUSION

Because your conclusion provides an opportunity to remind the audience of your main points and to help them remember what you have said, you need to prepare your conclusion as carefully as you did the body of your speech.

First, it is a good idea to signal to your audience that you have reached the conclusion of your speech so that they will focus on your final message. You can do so by using the following phrases:

in conclusion   in sum

to conclude   to summarize

by way of conclusion   to sum up

Now let's consider how you can structure your conclusion. The first part of a conclusion usually consists of a summary that serves as a reminder to the audience of the main points that you have covered and gives the speech a sense of completeness. In the speech "Are You Prepared for an Earthquake?" the summary part of the conclusion is:

To sum up, my advice to you is to make the simple preparations I have suggested and be sure you know what to do during and after an earthquake.

After summarizing your main points, you need to do something to help the audience remember the content of your speech. You can accomplish this in several ways: by referring back to something mentioned in the introduction, by including an illustration or personal experience, by appealing to the audience, or by using a quotation. One or more of these devices may be included in the same conclusion. For example, in the conclusion for "Are You Prepared for an Earthquake?" we can find examples of each of these ways of concluding a speech.

You may end up with no running water, no gas, no electricity; your phone line may be down. And emergency services will be assigned to areas that have the most serious damage. So help could be a long time in coming. This is exactly what happened after the earthquake in San Francisco. Emergency services were concentrated in the Marina district, which experienced the heaviest damage. In the meantime, other districts had to go without gas and electricity for several days before the utility company was able to restore these services. (*Reference to earthquake mentioned in the introduction*) My son was one of those who had this experience. It took four days before the electricity was restored to his apartment. (*Personal experience*)

Clearly, then, the more you are able to rely on your own resources when a major earthquake occurs, the better the chances are for

you and your family to survive! (*Appeal*) Remember the well-
known words of the boy scout motto—"Be prepared!"
(*Quotation*)

When giving your conclusion, you should try to express the last sentence, in particular, in such a way that you leave a strong impression of your
speech with the audience. Once you reach the end of your conclusion, don't
add any further comments. An audience tends to become impatient if a speaker
keeps adding more material after what appears to be the end of the speech.

Although the conclusion to the earthquake speech is written out so that
you can look at the way it is structured, we recommend that you prepare your
conclusion in outline form as you did for the body of your speech. Following
is an example of how this conclusion would be written in outline form:

I. Summary:

Make preparations

Know what to do *during* an earthquake

   after an earthquake

II. Possible effects of earthquake:

No running water, gas, electricity

Phone lines down

Lack of emergency services—assigned to most seriously damaged areas

III. Earthquake in San Francisco:

Services concentrated in Marina

Other districts—no gas and electricity for days

Son's experience

IV. Importance of relying on own resources—"be prepared"

Activity 8:   Evaluating Conclusions

Decide which of the following would make good conclusions. Be prepared to
make suggestions about how the others could be improved. Consider whether
each conclusion seems to provide an adequate summary of the main points of
the speech and whether it has an ending that the audience is likely to remember.

a. To conclude, these two techniques of self-defense that I've just
   shown you are only a beginning. You need to know much more

about how to protect yourself. Don't let yourself be attacked like my friend in the parking lot. I urge all of you to take a class in self-defense. Your life may depend on it.

b. As we've seen, a course in auto mechanics can be very valuable. I certainly benefited from taking one. So listen to my advice; don't wait any longer. Learn all you can about your car.

c. In conclusion, in order to be an effective tutor, you obviously need to be familiar with the subject you are tutoring in. You must spend time trying to figure out your tutee's strengths and weaknesses, and you should also be supportive and encouraging of your tutee's efforts to learn. In so doing, you will feel the great satisfaction that comes from helping others. And, at the same time, you will almost certainly broaden your own knowledge of your subject matter. Being an effective tutor, then, can certainly prove to be a rewarding experience.

d. You can see how easy it is to make a kite. So I hope you all have fun making your own kites.

e. To sum up, you can see how easy it is to learn to play the anklung in just a few minutes. So if somebody asks you if you can play a musical instrument, you can answer, "Yes, I can play the anklung." You can explain that the anklung is a traditional Asian bamboo instrument. And you can show them how to shake it properly in order to play a melody. Now you all know how to play at least one musical instrument, the anklung.

Activity 9:   Evaluating Your Classmates' Conclusions

For homework prepare the conclusion to your speech in an outline or on note cards. Then, in small groups, listen to and evaluate one another's conclusions. Listen more than once if necessary and give suggestions for improvement as needed. Here are some suggested questions for evaluation:

1. How does the speaker indicate that this is the conclusion?

2. Does the conclusion summarize the main points of the speech? What are the main points?

3. Does the conclusion end in a way that will make the audience remember the main focus of the speech?

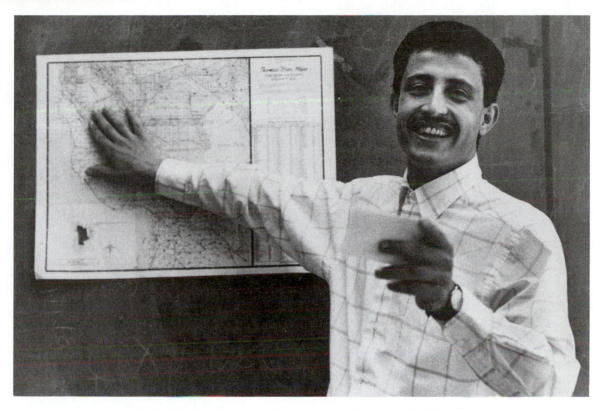

Get your audience involved right from the start with a strong introduction and a friendly approach.

PREPARING YOUR INTRODUCTION

In planning a speech, you usually prepare the introduction last. Preparing the body establishes for you exactly what you want to say about your topic, and the conclusion gives you the opportunity to bring your message home to your audience. Your final task is to think of a way to stimulate your audience's interest in your topic right from the beginning of your speech. It is your opening sentence that gives your audience their first impression of you as a speaker. Occasionally, people change their first impressions of a person over time, but in the course of a short speech, they have little opportunity to do so. Therefore, you should do your very best to create a positive first impression while preparing your audience for what you have to say. Most introductions do the following:

- catch the listeners' interest
- create a good rapport with the audience
- introduce the general topic of the speech
- move to the specific topic of the speech

You can follow this basic pattern for your introduction:

1. Begin with some sentences that gain your listeners' attention and that give some background information about your topic. This allows your listeners to start thinking about what you will say.

2. Begin to build a good relationship with the audience, that is, to create rapport.

3. Become more specific as you narrow your topic in order to focus the audience's attention on the topic.

4. State your specific topic directly in the last or next-to-last sentence of your introduction so that your audience will have no doubts in their minds about what your topic is.

Let's look at each of these points in more detail.

Catching the Listeners' Interest

Many people are not good listeners and will listen only if you interest them. Therefore, in the beginning of the speech, it is especially important to make your listeners interested, curious, and even excited about what you are going to say. With an introduction such as "Good morning. Today I'm going to talk about how to buy a guitar," you won't excite your audience much or encourage them to listen to you. To catch your listeners' interest, you might use one of the following techniques.

1. **Give your listeners a good reason to listen to you.** You can tell them that you will solve one of their problems or that you will give them valuable advice. You can give them any reason that you think will make them want to listen to you.

    EXAMPLE:

    If you're like me, you sometimes feel shy and nervous when you go on a job interview. You think maybe the interviewer won't like what you're wearing or what you say. Worse yet, you're afraid

Give your listeners a good reason to listen to you.

you won't have anything to say at all. Well, you don't have to be nervous anymore. If you follow just a few simple steps, you can be confident in all of your job interviews from now on.

The speaker knows that everyone probably feels nervous in an interview. The audience will listen to find out if the speaker has a solution to this problem. If the members of your audience feel that they will personally benefit by listening to you, they will listen.

2. **Ask the audience questions.** Questions are a good way to stimulate the audience's attention, but you must be careful not to overuse them. You may ask a question and accept a few individual responses from the audience. Another possibility is to *poll* the audience by requesting a show of hands as you ask the question (for example, "Let me see a show of hands—How many of you have ever felt nervous during a job interview?"). After asking this kind of question, you must pause to give the audience sufficient time to respond. Then you must be careful to acknowledge the response to your question before continuing with your speech.

   Another kind of question you can use is the rhetorical question, a question that you ask and then answer yourself. The purpose of this type of question is to involve the audience in what you are saying, to have them think of what their own answer to the question would be. You might consider that asking a question is an easy way for you to begin a speech, but to truly engage the audience, you have to put some thought into your question. An easy question to introduce a speech on playing the anklung would be "How many of you know how to play a musical instrument?" But here is a more thought-provoking question.

   > **EXAMPLE:**
   >
   > How many of you would learn to play a musical instrument if you could do so without putting in years of hard work? Probably almost all of you. You will then be happy to learn that not all instruments are hard to play. There is one easy instrument you can learn to play in just a few minutes; it's called the anklung, a traditional Indonesian bamboo instrument. It looks like this, and now I am going to show you how to play it. First, I will show you how to shake it to obtain different notes, and then I will teach you how to play a melody on it.

3. **Use a story to illustrate your main point.** Because everyone likes to listen to stories, this is a good way to get your listeners' attention. You can use a story about a famous person or one from personal experience, but *be careful!* Use your story only as an illustration of your main point. Don't make the story so long that everyone, including yourself, forgets the main point.

EXAMPLE:

One night, last year, a friend of mine was walking to her car. Suddenly she was attacked. She wasn't seriously hurt. In fact, she was more shocked and frightened than hurt. But this made me think about my own safety. I decided to take a class in self-defense. I found there are several basic ways people can protect themselves. Today, I'd like to show you two ways you can stop someone from attacking you.

The speaker uses the story of her friend to get the listeners' attention. Notice, however, that because the topic of the speech isn't the friend, she doesn't provide a lot of details about the attack. Although you can refer to the story later in your speech, remember that your story should only be used as an example of a point you are making.

4. **Keep your listeners in suspense.** Another way of arousing listeners' interest is to keep them guessing about your actual topic. However, you need to be careful that your unexpected topic logically follows from what you have said before. Don't, for example, begin your speech by explaining how to grow orchids and then discuss flower arrangement. Although your actual topic will be unexpected, it must relate to the first part of your introduction.

EXAMPLE:

Sometimes, we have trouble keeping busy. Hours, even days, are empty, and we can become bored. However, with a little thought and planning, we can fill up some of our empty time. We might take a walk, go to a movie, or read a book. Although these methods might take up a few extra hours, there is one way to make sure that every moment of our lives is full and busy. We can join the Army.

5. **Open your speech with a startling fact or statistic.** This is another way of grabbing the audience's attention at the outset. For instance, instead of mentioning the San Francisco earthquake, the earthquake speech might begin as follows:

EXAMPLE:

Maybe you think that you don't have to worry about earthquakes—they never happen where you live. But did you know that during 1990, 68 significant earthquakes occurred, and that more than 52,000 people were killed in those earthquakes?

Use whatever opening seems most appropriate for your speech, but always make sure that it clearly relates to your topic.

Creating a Good Rapport with the Audience

Everyone has had the experience of listening to a speech on an interesting topic but finding the speech itself boring. Why does this happen? One of the reasons could be that the speaker didn't build a good relationship with the audience; in other words, there was not a good rapport between the speaker and the audience. In order to make a speech more interesting, a speaker needs to involve the audience in the speech and work to overcome the invisible barrier between speaker and audience.

Good speech delivery contributes greatly toward creating a good rapport with your audience. Eye contact and sufficient volume are essential. Changes in facial expression, an occasional smile when it is appropriate, and gestures are also important. And an audience usually relates better to a lively speaker who visibly shows enthusiasm for the topic. In addition to appropriate speech delivery skills, you can use several other rapport-building techniques:

1. **Talk to the audience directly.** When you address the audience in this way using words such as *we, you,* and *your,* each person in the audience feels that you are speaking directly to him or to her (for example, "*We've* all experienced . . ." or "Did *you* ever wonder . . . ?").

2. **Identify a common experience.** When you say, "We have all experienced the anxiety . . . ," you are saying to the audience, "You and I are alike." Listeners will be more likely to listen to someone they identify with and feel a bond with.

3. **Ask the audience questions.** By asking the audience questions, you show that you care about the audience's opinions and ideas. Questions make a speech seem a little more like a personal conversation between the speaker and each member of the audience (for example, "Did you ever wonder . . . ?" or "And what do you think I found out?").

The following introduction contains examples of each of these techniques.

EXAMPLE:

I'm sure we've all experienced the anxiety that comes with starting a new job. On the first day of a new job, did you ever wonder if you could really do the job, if you could do it fast enough, if you could get along with your co-workers? Well, I have surveyed some of my relatives and friends about strategies they've used to help them cope with this anxiety. And what do you think I found out? Today, I'm going to share with you the guidelines I worked out from this survey that have really proved helpful to me. I'm going to explain how to succeed in a new job by being responsible, by showing initiative, and by cooperating with your co-workers.

Activity 10:   Noting Techniques for Creating Rapport

Look at the introduction examples on pages 88–91. Which of the following techniques does the speaker use to create a good rapport?

- addresses the audience directly

- identifies a common experience

- asks questions

Narrowing the Focus of Your Topic

A speaker normally begins a speech by catching the listeners' attention and introducing the general topic of the speech. From this first general reference to the topic in the introduction, the speaker then narrows the topic to the specific focus of the speech. Look at the following introduction and notice how the speaker begins with a general topic and narrows it to a more specific one.

(1) As college students, we have probably all needed help with our studies at one time or another; and maybe some of us have been able to help others too. (2) In my case, I helped my friends with their math and my friends helped me with my English. (3) Eventually, I realized I liked helping others besides my friends with math and could even get paid for it. (4) Now, if you have a strong background in one of your school subjects, such as math or chemistry, you might consider becoming a tutor—that is, you might get a job helping others learn one of these subjects. (5) Then, of

course, you would want to be as effective a tutor as possible.
(6) So, how can you become an effective tutor? Well, you must know your subject matter, you have to figure out your tutee's strengths and weaknesses, and you need to support and encourage your tutee.

In this introduction, note how the speaker does the following:

1. The first sentence gains the audience's attention and introduces the general topic of *students needing help with their studies.*

2. The second sentence suggests that the process of helping begins with *students helping each other.*

3. The third sentence moves to *helping students besides friends.*

4. The fourth sentence introduces the idea of *becoming a tutor.*

5. The fifth sentence limits the topic to *becoming an effective tutor.*

6. The sixth sentence, in the form of a question, clearly states the specific topic, and the response to the question sets out the plan for the speech.

Stating the Topic Clearly and Establishing the Plan for Your Speech

As you can see in the previous example, the question "So how can you become an effective tutor?" clearly states the topic of the speech. And the response, "Well, you must know your subject matter, you have to figure out your tutee's strengths and weaknesses, and you need to support and encourage your tutee," sets out the plan for the speech. The main points for the speech on how to become an effective tutor would then be:

I. Know subject matter

II. Figure out tutee's strengths and weaknesses

III. Support and encourage tutee

Having clearly heard the main points of your speech, the audience is then prepared for you to cover each of them in the order you specified.

In summary, think of the way you introduce your topic as a narrowing from general to specific like this:

> Introduce the general topic of the speech.
>
> Narrow the focus of the topic.
>
> State the specific topic and the plan.

We recommend that you prepare your introduction in outline form, as you did with the body and the conclusion of your speech. Following is a sample outline for the introduction to the speech "How to Become an Effective Tutor."

I. College students need help with studies
   Friends math—me English
II. Help others besides friends
   Math—got paid
III. You could become tutor
   Strong background in school subject
IV. How can you become an effective tutor? (statement of topic)
   Know subject matter
   Figure out tutee's strengths and weaknesses
   Support and encourage tutee

Activity 11: Noting the Specific Topic and the Plan for the Speech

Look at the introduction for the "How to Succeed in a New Job" speech on pages 92–93. Underline the sentence in which the speaker states the specific topic. Then identify how the speech will be organized.

Activity 12: Evaluating Introductions

Look at the following introductions. Some of them are well organized, progressing from general to specific, but others have problems. Which do you think are good? What is wrong with the ones that need improvement?

a. How many of you have ever gone skydiving? No one? Well, it's not surprising that none of you have ever tried it. Most people think that skydiving is a good way to get killed. In fact, skydiving is a very safe sport—if you get some training on the ground first. You will greatly reduce your chances of injury if you enroll in a good training program before you try to jump out of an airplane. A good training program will train you how to jump from the plane and how to land.

b. Your résumé should include information about your previous work experience, your education, any special skills or training you have, and your job objective.

c. If you have fat thighs, don't worry. There's a new weight-loss program called "Thinner Thighs in Thirty Days." And the author guarantees that in only thirty days you can reduce your thigh measurements. There are three parts to this program—the work-off, the walk-off, and the weigh-off. You only have to work six days at the program. On the seventh day, you can do something fun like go out to dinner or read a good book.

d. If you're like me, you sometimes have problems falling asleep at night. What do you do on those nights? Take a sleeping pill? Watch a late-night movie? Most of these traditional methods to fall asleep work only some of the time. Sleep experts, however, recommend two self-relaxation techniques that are guaranteed to work night after night. Today, I'm going to explain these two techniques to you.

e. What's your favorite outdoor activity? Well, as far as I'm concerned, there's nothing better than flying a kite. Flying a kite is great because it's easy to do and it doesn't cost much money. Of course, you can buy your kite, but kite flying is even cheaper if you make your own kite. Today, I'm going to help you save some money by showing you how to make a kite; I'll show you how to make first the body and then the all-important tail.

Activity 13:   *Listening to and Evaluating Introductions*

Your instructor will give four introductions for a speech on "Three Things You Should Know Before You Take a Photograph." The first main point in the speech will be "First, you should know about lighting"; thus, when you hear this, you will know the introduction is complete. Listen to the introductions and evaluate them according to the given criteria. Put a plus sign (+) next to the criteria that are successfully met.

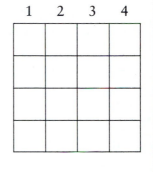

	1	2	3	4
Catches the listeners' interest				
Creates a good rapport with the audience				
Introduces the general topic of the speech				
Narrows the focus of the topic so that the specific topic and the plan of the speech are stated at the end of the introduction				

Activity 14:   *Preparing Introductions*

1. In small groups, consider how you could catch the audience's interest for each of the following speech topics:

   How to dress for a job interview

   How to write a résumé

   How to warm up before jogging

   How to give a successful party

2. Select *one* of these topics and, as a group, prepare an introduction.

3. Use the following questions to evaluate your introduction:

   a.   How does the opening attract attention?

   b.   How does the introduction create rapport?

   c.   What is the general topic of the speech?

   d.   Does the introduction narrow the focus of the topic?

   e.   What is the specific topic of the speech?

   f.   What is the plan for the speech?

4. Choose a group member to present your introduction to the class.

5. Be prepared to evaluate each group's introduction after it is presented to the class.

Activity 15:   Evaluating Your Classmates' Introductions

For homework prepare an introduction to your speech in an outline or on note cards. Then, in small groups, listen to and evaluate one another's introductions. Listen more than once if necessary, and give suggestions for improvement as needed. Use the questions in Activity 14 for evaluation.

USING VISUAL AIDS

As you prepare your speech, it is a good idea to think of the kinds of visual aids that would be appropriate for your topic. Visual aids serve several purposes. First, visual aids can help attract the audience's attention and add to the interest of the presentation. Second, they help to clarify information. For instance, if a speaker recites some statistics, it is difficult for listeners to retain them all. But if listeners see the statistics in the form of a graph while the speaker refers to them, they are more likely to retain them. Third, a visual aid that presents an outline of a speech helps listeners to remember the main points more easily than if they just hear them. To help you select appropriate visual aids, we have listed some of the most common types here and given some cautions for each.

Physical Objects

For some demonstrations physical objects are a must. For example, if you are demonstrating a Japanese tea ceremony or Chinese brush painting, you need to show the objects involved, especially because these are cultural items that your audience may have no knowledge of. To explain how something operates, you might use real objects or a model.

Cautions: Be sure that all members of the audience will be able to see the objects. This might mean providing large-scale replicas of the objects. If several objects are involved, display and discuss them one at a time to keep the audience's attention properly focused. However, if many objects are needed for a process that you are demonstrating, it is usually better to lay them all out at the beginning of your speech so that they are at hand when you need them. It is generally not a good idea to pass objects or pictures around the audience when giving your speech because people tend to focus on viewing the object or passing it to another person rather than giving their full attention to the speaker.

Handouts

Handouts are effective for presenting maps, charts, diagrams, complex information like technical definitions, or information you want the audience to take home with them (for example, some important statistics or a list of instructions for carrying out a task). A handout, such as a résumé, can also be effective for showing the format of a written document.

Cautions: Make sure that the parts are labeled (with numbers or letters) so that you can direct the audience's attention to them. A one-page handout should be sufficient for a short presentation. Providing the handout *during* the speech may interrupt the flow of your speech and may distract the audience. Thus, distribute the handout *before* the presentation if the content is necessary to understand the speech; distribute the handout *after* the speech if it is to serve as a reminder (for example, a recipe or a list of instructions). Remember that you lose eye contact when your audience is looking at a handout, so keep your handout as simple as possible. For an example of a simple handout, see Figure 3.1, "Shutter Speed Dial," on page 78.

Chalkboards

Chalkboards can be used for diagrams or outlines, although a well-prepared poster is both clearer and more attractive. However, the chalkboard is especially useful for writing down unfamiliar names or terms as well as important dates or numbers.

Cautions: Write on the board before the presentation, if possible. It is boring for the audience to sit and wait while you put your information on the board before or during your speech. If you must write during your talk, then (1) practice writing on the board ahead of time and (2) don't talk to the board while writing. When referring to something on the board, point at it with the hand closest to the item, face your audience, and don't stand in front of what you have written.

Make sure information on visual aids is large
enough for the audience to read it.

Posters

Posters can be exceptionally useful visual aids for outlines, diagrams, charts, and graphs. A poster is more effective than the chalkboard in that: (1) you can take time to prepare it properly before your presentation; and (2) you can make it more visually appealing by using a variety of colors, designs, and lettering styles. As with the chalkboard, you can point to the relevant information and keep the attention of the audience focused. Posters should be kept covered except when referring to the information they present; otherwise, they tend to distract the audience's attention from the speaker.

Cautions: Make sure the diagrams, numbers, or words on your poster are large enough for everyone to see. And, as with the chalkboard, be careful not to talk to the poster.

Overhead or Slide Projectors

Projectors also allow you to focus the audience's attention, although the audience can become more absorbed in what you are projecting than in what you are saying. For a short presentation it is best to show only a few key items on a projector. A particular disadvantage of using a slide projector is that the room must be dark, making it difficult for you to see your notes. Of course, this is not the case with an overhead projector. Should you choose to use a projector, you will need to prepare your materials and arrange to set up the equipment ahead of time.

Caution: Because a lot of time is required to set up a projector, don't try this aid for a short speech if you are not skilled at using it.

Cassette Players

You will need a cassette tape player for a demonstration requiring sound, such as music to accompany a demonstration of a dance step or a conversation between two people to accompany a demonstration of problems of personal interaction.

Cautions: Make sure your machine has sufficient volume for the room in which you are speaking. Also, before you begin your presentation, have the tape at the exact point where you wish to start it. You don't want to spend valuable presentation time searching on the tape for the sounds you want.

Audience Members

For some demonstrations it is appropriate to get the help of another individual. For example, if demonstrating a first-aid technique, you would want a "victim" to aid. If demonstrating a dance step, you might want a couple to do the step while you explain the movements. If demonstrating effective management techniques, you might want to have two people act out a difficult employee–supervisor situation. For other demonstrations it might be appropriate for the entire audience to participate in the demonstration (for example, by making a corsage or doing warm-up exercises). Having the entire audience take part is a good way to ensure comprehension and involvement.

Cautions: If using one or several other people, rehearse your presentation with them ahead of time. If using the entire audience, rehearse ahead of time using a friend or friends as the audience.

Remember that the key to effective use of audiovisual aids is careful preparation and practice. Whatever aids you choose, they should *add* to your presentation, not *distract* your audience's attention from it. In other words, don't make your aids so interesting or complex that the audience focuses on the aids and doesn't listen to what you are saying.

Activity 16:   *Choosing Appropriate Visual Aids*

Describe appropriate audiovisual aids for the following speech topics.

EXAMPLE

TOPIC: How to make an origami crane. (Origami is the Japanese art of folding paper to make flowers, birds, and other shapes.)

AIDS: Use a large-size origami paper (say 16 inches by 16 inches) for demonstrating. Provide origami paper for each member of the audience (say 6 inches by 6 inches). The audience will fold their papers individually following the speaker's instructions. Write on the chalkboard *crane* and *origami*. Show a picture of a crane.

1. How to write a business letter

2. How to give first aid

3. How to do a Greek folk dance

4. How to brush and floss your teeth properly

PRESENTING YOUR SPEECH

You can follow the steps given in "Practicing Your Oral Report" in Unit 2 to prepare for your speech. This time, practice using your visual aids to make sure that you can finish your speech within the allotted time.

When giving instructions or doing a demonstration, it is especially important that the audience be able to follow and understand each step. Thus, as you give your presentation, try to monitor your speaking in response to your audience's reactions. If your eye contact is good, you will, for the most part,

Practice makes perfect. This presenter's skill in demonstrating origami techniques results from extensive practice and contributes to a smooth presentation.

be able to see from the facial expressions of your audience whether they are able to follow you. What can you do if they appear confused?

1. Slow down if you think you may have been going too fast.

2. Back up: "Let me repeat the last point I made."

3. Paraphrase: "Let me say that in another way."

4. Give an illustrative example: "Let me give you an example of what I mean."

Should you make an error or perhaps stumble over your words, you can always apologize and say, "Excuse me. Let me say that again." It is a good idea to plan beforehand to explain any unfamiliar vocabulary, but you should also be prepared to explain other words if, at any point during the speech, you think that the audience doesn't understand.

In general, if you are successful in monitoring your audience's reactions, you will find they appreciate your concern and will be very willing to respond.

Listening and Evaluating

Before members of the class give their speeches, you will need to review the evaluation criteria on the form that follows Activity 17. As you evaluate a speech, listen carefully for the specific topic and the plan, which should include the main points. Check whether the speaker follows the plan and whether you can easily understand the information. Consider whether the visual aids are appropriate and whether the speaker is making good use of them. Finally, ask yourself if you would be able to follow the instructions or do the demonstration on your own after class.

Activity 17:   Reporting on an Instructive or Demonstration Speech

Choose the instructive or demonstration speech that you considered to be the best one. You may want to include the following in your report:

- an introduction in which you state whose speech you are evaluating and the topic of the speech

- reasons why the content of the speech made it an especially good one

- reasons why the delivery of the speech made it an especially good one

- a conclusion in which you summarize your reasons for selecting this speech as the best one and make a final comment

Unit 3   Instructions/Demonstration

Speaker _____

Evaluator _____

Topic _____

RATING SYSTEM: + = excellent
√ = average
− = weak

Content/Organization/Preparation

_____ Opening attracted listeners' attention.

_____ Topic was clearly stated in introduction.

_____ Information was easy to follow.

_____ Appropriate transitions connected the points.

_____ Speech had a suitable conclusion.

_____ Visual aids were effective.

_____ Content fit time limit.

Comments and suggestions for improvement:

Presentation/Delivery

_____ Eye contact

_____ Vitality

_____ Rapport with audience

VOICE CONTROL:

_____ Volume

_____ Rate

_____ Fluency

_____ Comprehensibility

Unit 4

Providing Information: Group Discussions and Presentations

SAMPLE GROUP DISCUSSION

In the following opening portion of a discussion, several students are talking about homelessness, a topic they have chosen for discussion, research, and an informative oral presentation.

RAUL: So, as the moderator, I guess it's my job to get us started. Maybe we could begin by just talking about why we chose this topic and what questions we have about the homeless.

KENJI: Okay, I'll start. I guess the thing that strikes me most is how many homeless people there are in this country. Before I came here, I had no idea there were so many people living on the streets. How long has this been going on? And I really want to find out why these people are living like this. Is it just the economy?

RAUL: You've come up with some good questions, Kenji. Now, what about you, Najwa?

NAJWA: Well, I've lived here a long time, but it seems to me that it's just been in the last five years or so that this problem has become so serious. And, like you Kenji, I'm also interested in the causes of homelessness. I've read that one cause is the lack of low-cost housing—there's just no place for poor people to go. But there must be lots of other causes as well.

RAUL: Yes, I'm sure there are. Anything else, Najwa?

NAJWA: Well, because I'm Palestinian, the issue of homelessness is never far from my mind. But I guess my concern here is to find out just who the homeless are—what their lives are like and what they think. I know lots of people say that the homeless are just too lazy to work or can't work because they're drug addicts or winos or crazy, but I'm sure there's more to it than that.

RAUL: Right, I've heard people say that, too. And they complain about the homeless being really aggressive about asking for money. There's a real backlash these days.

KENJI: What do you mean?

RAUL: Well, at first people were sympathetic to the problems of the homeless, but now they see the homeless taking over their parks and libraries and panhandling on their streets—they see the homeless as a threat, so they are reacting in an angry and hostile way. They're demanding that the government get these people off the streets—not because they want to help the homeless, but because the homeless are interfering with their lives.

KENJI: I see what you mean. I didn't realize there were so many bad feelings toward the homeless. I'd be interested in learning more about that. But what about you, Raul? How come you chose this topic?

RAUL: Well, I come from a city that has a lot of homeless people, but like you, Kenji, I never expected to see so many homeless people here. And now in the neighborhood where I live, there seem to be more and more homeless all the time. I'd like to find out why this is happening and what the city is doing to help.

NAJWA: Me, too.

RAUL: Okay. So let's see what we've come up with so far. We want to learn about why there are more homeless every day and just who the homeless are. Also, we're interested in the causes of homelessness and the solutions—what's being done and what can be done. And then this backlash issue. Does that seem to cover what we've said so far?

KENJI: Sounds right to me. Oh, I just thought of something else . . .

For Discussion

1. What duties is Raul carrying out in his role of moderator of the small-group discussion? Is he doing a good job? Why or why not?

2. Does the participation seem more or less equal in the discussion so far? If so, what techniques do group members use to accomplish this? If not, why?

3. Do the group members seem to be listening carefully to one another's comments? What examples can you cite to show that they are or aren't listening carefully?

PARTICIPATING IN SMALL-GROUP DISCUSSIONS AND GIVING PRESENTATIONS

This unit has a dual focus: participating in small-group discussions and presenting informative speeches. As you work in small groups to talk about topics that you are interested in, you will have a chance to become more effective participants in group discussions. As you gather information from outside sources and discuss this information, you will improve your ability to provide substantial content for your presentations. As you work together to plan your presentations, you will get additional practice in organizing and supporting ideas for effective communication with others. Finally, your group presentations will give you another opportunity to work on your public speaking, as well as give you a chance to develop skills in answering questions from your audience.

Small-group discussions can have different functions: they can serve to analyze and solve problems, or they can serve as a forum for sharing information and opinions. Whatever their goals, they seem to be part of everyone's life: whether you are participating in an office staff meeting, a student study group, a political action group, a neighborhood tenants' meeting, or a personnel committee, you need good speaking and listening skills to function in a productive way. You also need to be familiar with strategies you can use to get into the discussion and to have your ideas heard. In addition, you need to be aware of strategies for keeping the discussion relatively balanced among the group members.

Giving informative reports is also something most of us do in our lives: in academic settings students are often asked to report the results of their projects or to summarize information from outside sources. Beyond school, citizens may give committee reports, employees may report on projects or propose new projects, salespeople may give sales presentations, scientists may present research results to colleagues, and so on.

ASSIGNMENT: GIVING A GROUP PRESENTATION

This assignment involves working as a small group to prepare an informative speech and present it to the class. To complete this assignment you need to do the following:

1. Decide on a topic, and then find a group interested in this topic.
2. Discuss with your group what you know about the topic.
3. Gather useful materials to provide additional content for your discussion and report.
4. Discuss this new information, and then organize your report and select appropriate information.
5. Give the presentation as a group to the class (ten to twelve minutes), with each group member speaking for approximately the same length of time.

FINDING YOUR TOPIC

The first thing you need to do is come up with topics you are interested in talking about and learning more about; then you can find classmates who share your interest. The following lists of topics, organized by category, might give you some ideas of general topics. Keep in mind that the discussion and presentation will focus on *information*, not on your *opinions* about a particular topic.

ENVIRONMENT

recycling	acid rain	rain forests
global warming	air pollution	endangered species
toxic waste	population control	the Green Revolution

ENERGY

nuclear power	solar energy	hydroelectric energy

HEALTH

medical costs	nutrition and health	vegetarian diets
stress	anorexia	aerobic exercise
junk food	chiropractors	non-Western medicine
genetic engineering		

TECHNOLOGY

space travel	life on other planets	robots
animal experiments and medical research	organ transplants	virtual reality

EDUCATION

bilingual education	large-scale testing	computers and learning
high school dropouts	working students	
sex education		

FAMILY

divorce	teenage pregnancy	the changing American family
child/spousal abuse	care of the elderly	
poverty	pets	

ENTERTAINMENT

violence on TV	movie rating system	athletes' salaries

SOCIAL/POLITICAL CONCERNS

youth gangs	drug use/abuse	gun control
vandalism	rape/date rape	abortion
the death penalty	causes of racism	gay/lesbian rights
equal rights	affirmative action	the graying of America
homelessness	the peace movement	
government spending priorities	pornography	the United Nations
	foreign purchase of U.S. businesses	English-only laws
worldwide starvation		drunk drivers

Take five minutes or so to write down topics that you would be interested in that aren't on the lists. After you have thought up some new topics, look over the lists again and put a check mark next to those topics that you are interested in.

Put your suggestions for topics on the blackboard, and then add any that you suggest from the lists. Using the list on the board, write down two or three topics that you are willing to use as your topic for this unit. Your goal then is to find a group of three or four people in the class who share an interest in one topic. When you have done so, put your names beside the topic on the board.

KEEPING YOUR DISCUSSION ON TRACK

To participate effectively and to help your group's discussion go as smoothly as possible, you need to become familiar with certain principles and cultural conventions of small-group discussion. These include ensuring that group members all contribute, keeping the discussion focused on the topic, listening actively, and assigning specific roles to individual members.

Participating Fully

Your silence in a discussion may be interpreted by others as a lack of interest, a lack of knowledge or ideas, or an unwillingness to cooperate. Realistically, participation will not be exactly equal among members, but it is everyone's responsibility to contribute to some extent.

Everyone in a group discussion is expected to
participate equally.

It is also everyone's responsibility to see that all members get a chance to
talk. This means that you shouldn't monopolize the conversation but should
help others to participate. An obvious way to encourage participation is with
questions. You can ask general questions, such as "Henry, what ideas do you
have?" An even better technique is to ask more specific questions, such as
"Sophia, do you think we need more homeless shelters in our city?" If one
member is doing most of the talking, one tactful solution is to say, "Maria,
you seem to have a lot of good ideas on this topic, but we're going to run out
of time and we still haven't heard from Sophia and Henry."

Getting into the Discussion

The appropriate way to "get the floor," that is, to enter the discussion, will vary according to the setting you are in. For example, in some groups, members are expected to raise their hands and be called on before speaking. In other groups, members may ask questions and make comments without first raising their hands. Thus, you need to pay attention to what the accepted behavior is in your group. In your informal small-group setting here, simply speaking up is all that is required. If you find you have trouble getting into the discussion, some informal "openers" to begin your comment or question include the following:

> Well   Now   Of course   You know   You see

Other common "openers" may seek to either elicit or offer additional information:

ASKING FOR INFORMATION	GIVING SOME INFORMATION
May I ask a question?	May I add something?
I have a question (about that).	May I say something here?
Could I ask . . . ?	I have a point here.
I'd like to know . . .	I'd like to say something here.
	I'd like to comment on that.
	I might add that . . .

If you find it difficult to participate in discussions, several strategies might be helpful. First, come to the discussion prepared: give some thought to the topic, perhaps do some reading, and think of some questions you want answered. Ask those questions as part of your contribution to the discussion. Second, when someone else asks a question that you can answer, speak up and answer it. Share any information you have. Finally, be sure to say something early in the discussion; if you keep waiting to speak, sometimes it becomes more difficult to participate.

Keeping Contributions Relevant and Direct

The cultural conventions of participating in small-group discussions also extend to the way in which you make your point or say what you want to say. People from other cultures are often surprised at how direct Americans are in expressing their ideas. Such people may come from cultures in which the appropriate way to make a point is to lead up to it gradually, with many seemingly irrelevant introductory remarks, or to say what is meant in an indirect manner. This is generally not appropriate in an American academic or work setting. English has many idioms that express this cultural value of directness, including "Get to the point," "Out with it," "Don't beat around the bush," and "Let's get down to brass tacks." These expressions are somewhat informal and tend to indicate impatience at another's lack of directness, but they give you an idea of how native speakers of English sometimes feel when the speaker doesn't seem to be saying something relevant to the topic.

To be consistent with this cultural value of directness, therefore, you should carefully *choose* and *limit* your contributions in a discussion. You should stick to the point. If you have an idea that isn't directly relevant to the current topic but that you think might be useful to the discussion in some way, then introduce your comment with an explanation (for example, "This isn't directly related, but may be something we should consider . . .").

Showing How Ideas Are Related

The contribution you make in a discussion may be directly related to that of the speaker before you. The techniques for getting more information, giving encouragement, asking for repetition and clarification, restating, and interrupting that we talked about in the context of an interview are of course useful in a discussion, too. In addition, you can relate your contribution to a previous speaker's ideas by referring to already discussed ideas or by expressing agreement or disagreement.

Referring to previous ideas   When your point is related to something another participant has recently said or to a prior discussion, it is a good idea to say so directly. You can do this by restating a speaker's idea before giving yours:

> Ali said that . . . , and I'd like to add that . . .
>
> Remember that in our last discussion we made the point that . . . , so now . . .
>
> In other words, what you are saying is . . .
>
> If I understand you correctly, you believe that . . .

You can also refer to what a previous speaker has said:

> In line with what Sophia just said, I'd like to say . . .
>
> Going back to what Joe said earlier about . . .
>
> Well, if what you just said is true, then doesn't it follow that . . .

Expressing agreement   Another way to relate your contribution to that of a previous speaker is to express agreement. Expressing agreement also helps build group spirit: a speaker won't always realize that you agree unless you say so. Common expressions of agreement include the following:

Right.	That sounds good to me.
That's true.	Yes, I think that's true.
That's right.	Yeah, that's what I was thinking.
Exactly.	That seems logical.
I agree on that point.	You may be right.
I agree with what Henry said.	I do kind of agree that . . .
I think so too.	I think I'm pretty much in agreement with Sue that . . .
I don't think so either.	
You're right about that.	

Note that the last four expressions show *qualified* agreement. Which words express this?

Expressing disagreement   Although native speakers of English frequently do disagree, they generally do not use direct expressions of disagreement like "I disagree" or "No, you're wrong" except with very close friends or associates, or when they feel forcefulness is required. Such responses are inappropriate in most group discussions because they seem to represent an attack on a speaker's ideas. In order to express your disagreement, you can "soften" your response by using expressions like these:

Well, I wouldn't necessarily agree with that.

Hmmm. I see it somewhat differently.

Your view is slightly different from mine.

A common tactic is to state your own ideas without admitting that you disagree; the other participants will realize that you disagree. Such a contribution often takes a "Yes, but" form:

Yes, but I think . . .

That may be true, but don't you think . . . ?

Oh? Well it seems to me that . . .

That's interesting, but in my view . . .

Well, I feel that . . .

Listening Actively

Certainly, speaking is crucial in a small-group discussion, but understanding what others are saying is just as important. This means being an active listener and taking responsibility for comprehension. If you can't understand what another person is saying or don't see how it relates to the topic at hand, you have a duty to speak up and get clarification. This may mean interrupting the speaker; to do this you can use a polite opener such as the following:

Excuse me for interrupting, but . . .

Sorry to interrupt, but . . .

May I interrupt for a moment?

Excuse me, but . . .

Pardon me, but . . .

Eye contact is an important element of active listening, so you need to remember to look at speakers as they talk. Your attentiveness will give speakers confidence and perhaps even improve their speaking. In addition, don't distract speakers by actions such as tapping your pen, thumbing through your notebook, and so on.

Another aid to active listening, as well as to promoting a successful discussion, is taking brief notes as ideas come up in the discussion. You don't want to distract the speaker by continually writing, but you can balance your eye contact and note-taking by making a simple list of central points, key words, or questions that seem important to you. In addition to helping you concentrate on what the speaker is saying, these notes will provide a useful record of the discussion for later reference. If an item sparks a thought that you would like to contribute, put a check mark by it and you'll be more likely to remember it when you get a chance to speak.

Even while you are speaking you must still be an active listener. If someone interrupts you, you need to pay attention to the reason for it. If someone interrupts to ask you for clarification, find out what further information is needed and provide it. Then check to see if you've been successful. If someone interrupts to contribute an additional idea, you can keep talking, but do so politely by saying something like "Please let me finish."

When you are interrupted and later wish to resume speaking, you can use these expressions:

As I was saying . . .   To return to . . .

To get back to my point . . .   Going back to what I was
                                         saying . . .

Assuming Specific Roles

In a group discussion, all members share the responsibility for making the discussion successful. Everyone must be both a speaker and a listener. But if tasks related to managing and keeping track of the discussion are assumed by specific members, the group can sometimes be more efficient. Here are some possible roles:

- *Timekeeper:* watches the clock and makes sure all parts of the task get done in the time allotted
- *Recorder:* writes down the main points of the discussion and later organizes and reproduces these notes so that all members have a copy in subsequent discussions
- *Moderator:* opens the discussion, ensures equal participation among members, and manages the discussion

Acting as Moderator

The following are some suggestions for moderators.

Opening the discussion   As with interviewing, it is usually a good idea to begin with open-ended questions because they allow freedom in answering. If questions are too broad, however, they may be difficult to answer. For a discussion on homelessness, here are some sample questions:

OPEN ENDED: What has been your experience with homeless
              people here in this city?

TOO GENERAL: Why don't you begin by telling us what you know
              about homelessness.

Ensuring relatively equal participation   To encourage silent group members to speak, the moderator can ask direct questions such as the following:

Toshi, we haven't heard from you on this point. How do you see
the situation with regard to homeless shelters in our city?

When asking direct questions to draw out members, state the questions in such a way that they require information in the answer, rather than a simple yes or no. Questions that ask about opinions are also a good way to get others to talk. In addition to specific questions directed at quiet group members, more general directions may draw them out:

> Let's make sure we hear from everyone. I don't think we've heard from Toshi. Toshi?

The moderator is also responsible for cutting off a talkative group member who is dominating the discussion. One way to do this is to ask the talkative speaker a focused question, listen to the response, and then open the discussion to others. Here is an example:

> KOSTAS: . . . One of the biggest problems with the homeless situation is the large number of alcoholics and crazy people on the streets.
>
> MODERATOR: (*breaking in*) Excuse me, Kostas, but do you know what percent of the homeless fit that category?
>
> KOSTAS: Well, no, I don't have the exact figures, but I know . . .
>
> MODERATOR: (*breaking in again*) Just a moment. Does anyone have information about this?

Another technique for dealing with a talkative group member is to focus on procedure. Here are some things a moderator could say:

> You've made some very interesting points. Let's hear what the rest of the group thinks about them before we go on.

> Can you wait a minute before you expand on that point? It's an important issue and others have some reactions here, I'm sure. We'll get back to you in a minute.

> Excuse me, but the timekeeper has just signaled me that we have only ten minutes left, and we still have to cover several more points.

The moderator can also use summarizing as a technique to ensure equal participation. A summary could be introduced in this way:

> I'm sorry to cut you off, but I think we need to see where we're going at the moment, so I'll try to summarize the last few points.

The moderator can then conclude the summary by directing a question at a less talkative member.

The moderator needs to deal with talkative members tactfully; if such members sense that their ideas are not valued, they may stop contributing to the discussion and the group will suffer. The moderator also needs to monitor his or her own contributions to the group, being careful not to dominate the discussion or to engage in one-to-one conversations with group members. Ideally, discussion in the group is spontaneous, and members should feel free to speak up at any time, not just in response to the moderator.

Managing the discussion   The moderator can keep the discussion focused on the topic by two strategies: asking questions and summarizing. Sometimes group members talk on a very general level and accept statements without supporting information. Here, like an interviewer, a moderator needs to ask for more information and support. The moderator might say:

> That seems like an important point. Do you have some examples
> or statistics to back that up?

The moderator may need to ask about or make explicit connections between points as well, using questions such as these:

> Are you saying that cuts in welfare programs have been the main
> cause of homelessness?

> How does the information you've given us on the increasing num-
> ber of homeless shelters relate to these possible solutions to the
> problem of homelessness?

Summarizing can be used throughout the discussion to describe points that have been made or to call attention to questions that remain unanswered. Here are some possible comments:

> We've been talking about the causes of homelessness for a while,
> and we seem to have several main points. Let me state them and
> see if we're agreed and ready to move on to another issue.

> Are we through talking about our personal experiences with
> homeless people? If so, I'll sum up the points we've made.

The moderator will also have to deal with any conflicts that may occur among group members. The moderator should remain neutral, not taking sides with one of the people involved in the conflict. One strategy the moderator can use is to interrupt the speaker to focus on the ideas being discussed. He or she can point out the process that is going on rather than focusing on the individuals engaged in the conflict. The moderator might say something like this:

> Excuse me, but I need to jump in here to comment on what I see going on. We seem to have some disagreement on the best way to proceed in structuring our report. Of course, it's not surprising that we don't always agree on everything—after all, we're such brilliant students that great minds like ours are bound to disagree occasionally! So, it seems that one idea is to begin our report by talking about the extent of the homeless problem, giving statistics. Another idea is to begin with some biographies of homeless people. Perhaps we could discuss the pros and cons of each, and then we can decide which will be the most effective opening.

Activity 1: *Reviewing Some Points about Small-Group Discussions*

As a whole class or in small groups, discuss answers to the following questions. After you have discussed all thirteen, evaluate your discussion in terms of these features of effective discussions: full participation, relevant contributions, and active listening.

1. What are some differences between whole-class and small-group discussions?

2. Which of the principles would apply to whole-class discussions?

3. What topics are best dealt with in small-group discussion?

4. What is the best number of people for a small-group discussion? Why?

5. What responsibilities do all participants have in a small-group discussion?

6. How is it possible to ensure that *all* participants in the group contribute their ideas?

7. What is a good way to enter a small-group discussion when others have been talking? What do you say when you want to talk?

8. How can the group stay focused on the main discussion topic? What can you say when a member or members of the group begin to stray off the topic?

9. Why is it a good idea to show how your point relates to that of another group member? How can you do this?

10. What does it mean to be an active listener in the context of a small-group discussion?

11. What examples of poor group discussion etiquette have you noticed? How did group members respond? Think of examples of discussions that got out of control or were unproductive. Tell what happened in those cases.

12. What do you think about the idea of assigning special roles to group members (for example, moderator, timekeeper, recorder)? Would these roles be appropriate for all group discussions? What might be some problems with such roles? What other roles could you assign, or how might you reorganize these roles?

13. What are the duties of a moderator? Have you ever been the moderator of a group discussion? If so, what did you enjoy about the role? What was difficult about it?

EXPLORING YOUR TOPIC

In the opening part of the group discussion, it is important to give and listen to *all* ideas uncritically. This stage of offering ideas freely without criticizing or evaluating is commonly known as brainstorming. Often one person's idea will stimulate the thinking of others. You could begin by talking about why you chose this topic. Refer to information you have read or heard about your topic. Talk about your own personal experience as it relates to the topic. Don't forget to jot down ideas as they come up so that you can refer back to them for further discussion.

You might then want to explore areas of the topic in a more systematic way by breaking the topic down into component parts and seeing what you know about these parts. For example, if you were discussing the homeless, you might come up with these subtopics:

history of homelessness in the United States

numbers of homeless at the international, national, and local level

causes of homelessness

kinds of people that are homeless

personal feelings about homelessness

Who are the homeless? For a group discussion and presentation on the homeless, you will need to find answers to questions such as this.

Americans' opinions on homelessness

current actions to combat homelessness

potential solutions to homelessness

After discussing what you already know, you need to decide what kind of additional information you are interested in finding, because part of this assignment involves drawing on outside sources of information for your report. For example, on the topic of homelessness, you may choose to limit your topic to homelessness in the United States. You might then decide that you would like to find more information on four questions that seem interesting and important to you:

How extensive is this problem, that is, how many homeless are there?

What are some reasons that people are homeless?

What are the attitudes that people have about the homeless (including the attitudes of the class)?

What is being done/can be done to help the homeless?

Finding Additional Information

When looking for information on a topic, you will normally explore three major kinds of materials: reference works (for example, encyclopedias, almanacs, and abstracts), magazine or newspaper articles (especially to obtain the most current information), and books (especially to obtain more in-depth information). Interviews can provide additional information; experts at your school or public officials are possible interviewees.

One possibility is to go to the library as a group and check the *Readers' Guide to Periodical Literature* or a computerized magazine/newspaper index for relevant articles. These indexes will list various subtopics, and you can see which seem of interest to the group and then possibly assign different articles to different group members. However you divide up the work, you should end your first discussion session with a clear plan for getting additional information.

Working with Outside Sources

A computerized index used to locate helpful newspaper or magazines articles could give you information such as that shown in Figure 4.1. Which of these articles do you think would be most appropriate for our sample discussion on homelessness? Why?

Once you locate relevant articles, it is a good idea to photocopy them so that you can identify key points or questions by underlining or highlighting and also by writing in the margin. Remember to write down important reference information about your source articles, such as the author, title, name of the publication, date of publication, volume number, and page numbers. The excerpts on pages 126–128 are from articles related to our sample topic of the homeless. These excerpts have been marked as they might be in preparation for a group discussion on our four basic questions:

How many homeless are there?

What are some reasons for homelessness?

What attitudes do people have about the homeless?

What is being done or can be done to help the homeless?

Figure 4.1   Sample from Computerized Index

Magazine Index

HOMELESSNESS
 -causes of

> Would they be better off in a home? Why do people become homeless? by Laurence Schiff il   v42
> *National Review* March 5 '90 p33(3)

> Four causes of homelessness, by Peter M. Jones il   v121 *Scholastic Update* Feb 10 '89 p12(2)

HOMELESSNESS
 -International cooperation

> Global Strategy for Shelter for All by Year 2000 asked at climax of International Year. il   v25
> *UN Chronicle* March '88 p83(1)

HOMELESSNESS
 -Personal narratives

> Why I am homeless, by C.C. Bruno il   v49 *The Humanist* May–June '89 p10(3)

HOMELESSNESS
 -Public opinion

> Frustration, anger mark growing 'class war' in America. (homeless face backlash) by Sarah Ferguson il   v26 *National Catholic Reporter* May 11 '90 p3(1)

Look at the marginal notes and the underlinings. How do they relate to our four questions? Make a list of key words or expressions in the underlined portions that you do not fully understand or that you think might have to be explained to group members.

Excerpt from article 1 (Jones, 1989)*

4 factors cause homelessness

America is the wealthiest nation in the world. So why do as many as 3 million Americans currently suffer the pain of homelessness? Experts debate the causes of homelessness, but most point to <u>four interrelated factors: poverty, federal budget cuts, a lack of afford-able housing, and inadequate care for the mentally ill.</u>

(#1) **MORE PEOPLE LIVE IN POVERTY**

The main reason people are homeless is that they don't have enough money to pay for food, rent, and other basic necessities. Today, more Americans than ever have jobs. Yet, as the chart at the right shows [chart below], a growing number of Americans are also living below the poverty level.

Number of Americans Below the
Poverty Line (in millions)

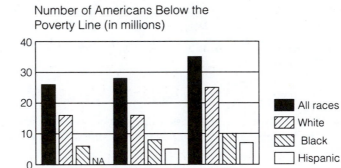

Source: U.S. Bureau of the Census.

Percent Rise in Federal Budget for
Social Welfare Programs

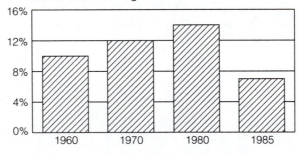

Source: U.S. Social Security Administration.

---

* "Four Causes of Homelessness," by Peter Jones. UPDATE, 2/10/89. Reprinted by permission of Scholastic Inc.

Why are so many living in poverty? One reason, experts say, is that many of the jobs created in recent years pay low wages. The minimum wage, set by Congress in 1981, is $3.35 an hour. But a person who earns the minimum wage and works a 40-hour week makes less than $7,000 a year. That's almost $5,000 less than the poverty level—the minimum amount needed to feed, clothe, and shelter a family of four.

low paying jobs

check this

Experts say a growing number of the nation's homeless—maybe 30 percent—have jobs. Yet, with the cost of living rising, these people simply can't make ends meet.

30% have jobs

#2 FEDERAL AID HASN'T KEPT UP

Many poor people rely on federally funded programs for food, rent, medical care, and other needs. But, as the graph at the right shows [graph above], the increase in the federal budget for social-welfare programs has fallen dramatically in recent years. . . .

↓ welfare programs

Excerpts from article 2 (**Manning, 1989**)*

The homeless who live in the shadow of Bush's new residence are among the estimated 3 million Americans who may be without shelter for one or more nights during the coming year. "The growing phenomenon of homelessness," says a report from the National Academy of Sciences, "is nothing short of a national disgrace."

How many? est. 3 million

Attitude: — a disgrace — of Bush

President Bush says he wants to take action. "I'd like to feel we would address [homelessness] with sensitivity and compassion," he said last December. . . .

Meanwhile, advocates for the homeless—and their allies in Congress—are gearing up for a major campaign to force the Bush administration to do more. "The federal government must declare war on the homeless problem," says Mitch Snyder, a Washington, D.C.–based advocate for the homeless. "Simple justice and decency demand no less."

Pressure on Bush adm.

Attitude: — homeless advocate

To figure out what needs to be done, it's important to understand a recent shift in government policy toward housing the poor. Almost every expert agrees that the key to solving homelessness is to build more housing. . . .

Solution: more housing

---

* "Is the Government Doing Enough to End Homelessness?" by Steven Manning. UPDATE, 2/10/89. Reprinted by permission of Scholastic Inc.

Excerpts from article 3 (Ferguson, 1990) *

attitude:
class war

In streets and doorways across the country, a class war is brewing between angry indigents and disgruntled citizens forced to step out of their way. . . .

people losing patience

"The tension level is definitely rising," says Wendy Georges, program director for Berkeley's Emergency Food Project. "With more homeless in the streets, people are starting to lose patience—even in Berkeley. If a city like this successfully attacks homeless people and homeless programs, it will set precedents. The homeless backlash will become a popular thing—so that nobody has to feel guilty about it."

why?
① ↑ numbers

Part of the reason for the growing backlash is simply sheer numbers. The U.S. Conference of Mayors' annual survey found that the demand for emergency shelter in 27 cities increased an average of 25 percent in 1989, compared to 1988, when demand increased 13 percent. About 22 percent of those requesting emergency shelter were turned away.

② change to younger & minorities

Public disfavor may also be spurred by changes in the makeup of the homeless population. Although figures are scarce, anyone who walks the streets can see that the homeless population has grown younger. A 1960 survey by Temple University of Philadelphia's skid row found that 75 percent of the homeless were over age 45, and 87 percent were white. In 1988, 86 percent were under age 45, and 87 percent were minorities.

ORGANIZING YOUR PRESENTATION

After preparing your outside sources, the first goal of the group will be to decide which points are the most promising for your report. The most promising would be those that seem interesting and important to you and those that you have a lot of information about. Then you will have to select supporting details.

---

* Ferguson, Sarah, "Frustration, Anger Mark Growing 'Class War' in America," *National Catholic Reporter,* Vol. 26, May 11, 1990, p. 3. Reprinted by permission of Sarah Ferguson, of the *National Catholic Reporter,* P.O. Box 419281, Kansas City, MO 64141, and of Pacific News Service.

Organize your ideas: Discuss the information you have found, consider which points to include in your presentation, then decide on the order of those points.

Organizing the Main Points

Once you have established your main points, you need to find a good way to organize them. As we pointed out in Unit 3, there are many ways to organize. Probably the most common method of organizing is according to main ideas, a method that can sometimes incorporate other types of organization within it. Recall that this type of organization was used in Unit 3 for the speeches on earthquakes and photography. For the discussion and report on the homeless, our four questions could easily serve as the basis for the four main ideas of the presentation.

The next step is to figure out what points to make about these main ideas. These four points could be selected:

1. the number of homeless—increasing rapidly

2. four causes of homelessness: poverty, federal budget cuts, a lack of affordable housing, and inadequate care for the mentally ill

3. attitudes toward the homeless—decreasing sympathy and growing hostility

4. solutions—more U.S. government involvement

The next task is to work out the best order for these points. In this case the original order seems to be a good one for several reasons. First, points 1 and 2 provide necessary background information on the topic. Although points 1 and 2 could be reversed because one doesn't depend on the other, the information in point 1 is more dramatic and thus might grab the audience's attention. Second, points 3 and 4 depend on the information in points 1 and 2 about the great increase in and causes of homelessness. Finally, this order follows a logical problem-solution sequence: points 1, 2, and 3 describe the problem of homelessness; point 4 talks about the solutions.

After you have decided on the order of your points, your group can decide who will present each point. All group members should present at least one main point.

Activity 2: *Organizing Main Points for a Presentation*

Consider the main points listed for each of the following speech topics. Number these points in what you consider to be the best order. Be prepared to defend your ordering.

a. Topic: Drunk Driving

    _____ laws in this state

    _____ possible solutions

    _____ number of deaths and injuries caused by drunk drivers

    _____ attitudes: police, MADD (Mothers Against Drunk Driving), teenagers, general public

b. Topic: Mother Teresa

    _____ winning the Nobel Prize

    _____ contribution to the world

_____ childhood and education

_____ recent work in various countries

_____ work in Calcutta

c. Topic: The Destruction of the Rain Forests

_____ effects of the present rate of destruction

_____ reasons for the cutting of rain forests

_____ efforts being made by environmental groups

_____ location and size of major rain forests throughout the world

Activity 3:   *Evaluating Main Points and Their Order*

When your group has decided on the main points for your presentation and the order in which the group will present them, list them on the board and get reactions from the class. The class can discuss these questions:

1. Do the main points seem equally related to the topic?
2. Is the order of the points appropriate?

Selecting Supporting Details

Your next task is to select information to support the points you will make. It is the supporting details that make a presentation interesting and convincing to an audience, so you need to choose them carefully. You can use details from your own experiences and/or from your outside sources as support. For example, if you were reporting on the increasing numbers of homeless people in the United States, you would want to cite facts and statistics from outside sources to prove that the numbers are large and increasing. Four common types of supporting information that you may wish to use in your report are summaries, examples and explanatory information, statistics, and quotations.

Summaries   As you read through your outside sources and look over your discussion notes, you may find that you want to summarize information to

Give careful consideration to your selection of
information for supporting details.

use in support of your main points. **Summarizing** means selecting and reporting on important ideas of a body of information. Thus, a summary is essentially a shorter version of something you read or hear that focuses on important ideas, not minor details. Three points to keep in mind when summarizing information are the following:

1. As when restating—paraphrasing—*use your own words* in a summary, not the exact words of the author or speaker.

2. As with a paraphrase, *identify* the source of the information.

3. In summarizing, be very careful that you *do not change* the author's or speaker's ideas and that you *do not add* your own ideas.

The length of a summary can vary. In its shortest form, a summary can be a single sentence. A very detailed summary might be as much as one-fourth as long as the original written or spoken text.

EXAMPLES:

As part of our discussion, we talked about our individual experiences with homeless people. I'd like to summarize part of our discussion so you can compare our experiences and attitudes with your own. All four of us regularly see homeless people on a daily basis, either at school, or at the bus stop, or on our neighborhood streets. Three of our group feel nervous when approached by the homeless for money, but all four of us usually give money to them. We all feel that the federal government should be doing more to help homeless people throughout the country.

Apparently, not everybody wants to help the homeless. According to a recent article by Sarah Ferguson in the *National Catholic Reporter*, there is a growing public backlash against the homeless. What is the cause of this new negative attitude about the homeless? Ferguson gives two possible reasons: the rapidly increasing numbers of homeless people and the changing composition of the homeless population—there are now more younger people and more minorities among the homeless.

Activity 4:   Summarizing Information

Working in groups, prepare a brief summary of the following excerpt. Hints on the task:

1. Underline the sentence or sentences that seem to contain the main idea.

2. State the idea out loud in your own words as though explaining it for someone who hadn't read it. Then write it down.

The completed summaries can then be written on the board and critiqued, paying attention to these points:

1. Does the summary, in fact, contain the main idea(s) of the text?

2. Does it contain only the original author's ideas, or has other information been added?

3. Has the group paraphrased the information, or does the summary stick too closely to the original wording?

> The sometimes belligerent attitude of street people goes along with a growing shelter and welfare rebellion. In New York, the growth of the Tent City in Tompkins Square reflected the refusal by many homeless to enter New York's degrading shelter system. As many as 1,000 people a night are housed in armories where contagious diseases like AIDS and tuberculosis run rampant. Moreover, a substantial number of homeless people refuse to sign up for welfare and other entitlement programs, preferring to fend for themselves on the streets rather than get caught up in a "dependency mentality" and suffer the degradation of long welfare lines and condescending case workers.*

Examples and explanatory information   If you were to make the point "The homeless in America come from many walks of life," don't think that your audience would automatically know exactly what you mean. Some might think that you mean some homeless are educated and some are uneducated; others might think that you are referring to different social classes; still others might think you mean different ethnic minorities. Your audience will understand you better if you give an example or explain in more detail exactly what you mean.

In the following excerpts from a speech, note how the speaker is using examples and explanatory information for supporting details. What are the details that the speaker has used? How does the speaker identify the source of the information?

EXAMPLES:

> The homeless in America today come from many walks of life. Many of us think of the homeless as being drunks, drug addicts, and mentally unbalanced people. And it's true that these types of people are among the homeless. But the homeless population now includes single women with families, elderly people living on fixed incomes, and people whose jobs pay so poorly that they can't

---

* Ferguson, Sarah, "Frustration, Anger Mark Growing 'Class War' in America," *National Catholic Reporter,* Vol. 26, May 11, 1990, p. 3. Reprinted by permission of Sarah Ferguson, of the *National Catholic Reporter,* and of Pacific News Service.

afford housing. The four articles we have told you about all mentioned the variety of types of people who make up the homeless population today.

In various parts of the U.S., cities are taking steps not to help the homeless, but to clamp down on them. In an article written in 1990 on attitudes toward the homeless, Sarah Ferguson gives these examples. In Washington, D.C., the city council has recently cut the homeless budget by nearly $20 million. In Atlanta, Georgia, the mayor has proposed a program to license panhandlers—that would mean a person couldn't beg others for money without this license. And in Berkeley, the University of California has sent police to clear the homeless out of a nearby public park on numerous occasions.

Statistics   Statistical information consists of numbers, percentages, and other measures. This kind of specific detail is useful because it is very clear and precise. If you said, "Many of the homeless actually have jobs," it would be unclear how many people you mean. Does "many" mean half of the homeless? Most of the homeless? On the other hand, if you said, "It is estimated that 30 percent of the homeless actually have jobs," your audience would have a clearer idea of how many people you are talking about.

Notice in the following example how the statistical information clarifies and strengthens the speaker's points. How are the sources of the statistics identified?

EXAMPLE:

There seems to be no question that the numbers of homeless are increasing. In a study done in twenty-seven American cities by the U.S. Conference of Mayors, as reported by Ferguson, it was found that in 1988 there was a 13 percent increase in the demand for shelters and in 1989 there was a 25 percent increase in the demand.

Along with the increase in the numbers of homeless there is another change: the homeless population has changed from older, white people to younger, minority people. Let's compare some statistics for 1960 and 1988 for the city of Philadelphia. In 1960, according to a survey done by Temple University and reported in Ferguson's article, 75 percent of the homeless were older than 45, and 87 percent of the homeless were white. And in 1988, 86 percent were younger than 45 and 87 percent were minorities.

Quotations   A quotation is the use of someone else's words. If you quote those words exactly, then you are using a direct quotation and should make that clear to your audience. If you restate the idea in your own words, then you are making an indirect quotation, or paraphrasing. In a speech, we frequently paraphrase another speaker or writer's exact words so that we can make the ideas more comprehensible to our audience. This is especially important when taking information from written sources because language meant to be *read* is often quite different from language meant to be *heard*.

Look at the following examples, in which the speaker uses direct quotation. How is the direct quotation identified? How is the source of the quote identified?

EXAMPLES:

In her recent article in the *National Catholic Reporter,* Sarah Ferguson discusses the anger that the homeless issue is provoking. In her words, quote, "a class war is brewing between angry indigents and disgruntled citizens forced to step out of their way."

But what do the homeless themselves think about the role that the government should play in finding solutions to the problem? Let me quote the words of Mitch Snyder, a well-known advocate of the homeless cause. According to Snyder, quote, "The federal government must declare war on the homeless problem. Simple justice and decency demand no less," end of quote. Many homeless people agree with Mr. Snyder.

In a recent article describing several homeless people, reporter Naomi Marcus introduces us to a homeless man in San Francisco. She gives us this vivid description: "Joseph Charles Moose is feeling all right this January morning. He has a bottle of Night Train wine in a paper bag on his lap, and he just had a good night's sleep in the boiler room under an Italian bakery near San Francisco's Fisherman's Wharf. He is holding a transistor radio and humming along, waving to friends from his perch on top of a park bench." *

---

* "The Many Faces of America's Homeless" by Naomi Marcus. UPDATE, 2/10/89. Reprinted by permission of Scholastic Inc.

You wouldn't ordinarily use a direct quotation that is as long as the one in the last example: one sentence is about the limit for a direct quotation. However, this quotation is good because it is very descriptive and is written in simple enough language to be easily understood. When you are deciding whether to use a particular direct quotation, try reading it aloud to your group to see if they can understand it. If not, then you should paraphrase it in simpler language.

Citing your sources   Whenever you use the words or ideas of another person or any information from an outside source such as an article, a book, or a newspaper, you must identify the source of that information. If you do not do so, your audience will think the ideas you report are yours. Failure to identify a source is known as plagiarism, and it is considered a serious offense.

Various methods of identifying sources are possible. We suggest that the first time a group member uses a source in a presentation it should be cited more fully. Give the author's full name, as well as the date and name of the magazine, newspaper, or book if it seems relevant. Then, when the source is used later in the speech, only a brief identification is needed.

FIRST TIME:

In an article written in 1990 on attitudes toward the homeless, Sarah Ferguson gives these examples . . .

In a recent article describing several homeless people, reporter Naomi Marcus introduces us to a homeless man in San Francisco. She gives us this vivid description . . .

LATER USE:

. . . according to a survey done by Temple University and reported by Ferguson . . .

As reported in Ferguson's article . . .

The four articles we have told you about all mentioned . . .

Activity 5:   *Analyzing Supporting Details*

Read the following excerpt in which a speaker is providing supporting details on one cause of homelessness and then do the following:

1. Find sentences or phrases that provide these kinds of supporting details: examples or explanatory information, statistics, and direct quotation.

2. Note where and how the speaker identifies the source of the information.

3. Describe the visual aids the speaker is using to help make the information clear.

4. Compare this speech segment to the excerpt on page 126 (most of the information the speaker uses comes from this excerpt). Select one example to show how the wording in the original article has been restated—paraphrased—in the speaker's own words to make it easier for the listener to understand.

There are four major causes of homelessness in America, according to Peter Jones in a 1989 article appearing in *Scholastic Update*. I have listed these on the board and will tell you about each of them. They are: poverty, federal budget cuts, a lack of affordable housing, and inadequate care for the mentally ill.

Let's first talk about poverty as a cause of homelessness. Jones points out that one reason for the increasing number of homeless is that more people than ever before are living below the poverty level. If you look at this chart I've prepared, you can see that the poverty level is here, at $12,000 a year. As the chart shows, the number of people below the poverty line increased from 25 million in 1979 to 33 million in 1986.

Now, Jones points out that one of the causes of this growing number of poor people is low-paying jobs. Why are there so many low-paying jobs? One reason is that many new jobs that have been created pay the minimum wage or only slightly better. Think of all the new jobs in the fast-food industry, for example, cashiers at McDonald's or cooks at Pizza Hut. These jobs pay the minimum wage. So here's the problem: a person who works for forty hours a week at the minimum wage falls right here on the chart. As you can see, this is well below the poverty level of $12,000 a year. In Jones's own words and I quote, "Experts say a growing number of the nation's homeless—maybe 30 percent—have jobs. Yet with the cost of living rising, these people simply can't make ends meet."

Activity 6:   *Adding Supporting Details*

The following general statements could be used in a speech on homelessness. For each statement, give one or more additional statements to support the point. Use information from the excerpts on pages 126–128 as suggested. Be sure to cite the sources of your information.

a. A second reason for the increasing number of homeless is decreased spending by the federal government on social welfare programs. (Hint: Use the second graph in article 1.)

b. The number of homeless people in the U.S. is growing. (Use article 2.)

c. Last December President Bush expressed his concern for the homeless. (Use article 2.)

d. People seem to be losing patience with the homeless they see around them, according to Ferguson. She suggests two reasons for this "homeless backlash." (Use article 3.)

PLANNING THE CLOSING, OPENING, AND TRANSITIONS BETWEEN SPEAKERS

In Unit 3, you learned about ways to conclude a presentation. For your group presentation, the final speaker should conclude by providing a summary of the main points. The speaker may wish to add some final comments on the value of the information presented.

Activity 7:   *Evaluating Conclusions*

Listen as your teacher or a classmate reads the following conclusions from a speech on homelessness to you. What is wrong with any that you think need improvement? Consider whether each conclusion seems to provide an adequate summary of the main points of the speech and whether it has an ending that the audience is likely to remember.

a. As we hope we've pointed out, the problem of homelessness seems to be increasing in this country. This is largely due to people's inability to find affordable housing, their low levels of income, the federal cutbacks in welfare programs, and the closing of institutions for the mentally ill. This increase in the homeless population, along with a shift to a younger, more ethnically diverse homeless population, is leading to new hostile attitudes on both sides: the homeless themselves and the average person who sees the homeless everywhere. The solution to this "class war," as it has been called, seems to lie with increased federal attention to providing more housing and reinstating welfare programs. It is our hope that the president will place the problems of the homeless high on his agenda of national concerns. Thank you for your attention. We're ready now to take any questions you may have.

b. Well, I guess that's all that my group has to say about the topic of homelessness. We hope you'll all go out and do something to help these people. The next time you see one, perhaps you'll be a little more sympathetic. Thanks for your attention. Now, are there any questions?

c. On behalf of our group, I would like to say in conclusion that we learned a great deal from our discussion and from our reading on this topic. It forced us to change our stereotypic view of the homeless and of their difficulties. We hope we have conveyed to you the seriousness and complexity of this problem; and we hope that you, too, have new insight into and compassion for the homeless as a result of our report. Now, we'll be happy to try to answer any questions you have for us.

In Unit 3, you also learned about ways to introduce your speeches, such as getting the listeners' attention with a question or giving them a good reason to listen to you. You might review that information before doing Activity 8.

Activity 8:   *Evaluating Introductions*

Listen as your instructor or a classmate reads the following introductions to a speech on homelessness aloud to you. Which of these introductions do you find interesting? What is wrong with the ones that you think need improvement? Consider whether each meets the criteria for a good introduction—that is, it grabs the listener's attention, it creates rapport, and it makes the specific topic and plan clear.

a. We'd like to begin our talk today by introducing you to a man named Joseph Charles Moose. You've probably never heard of him. He's one of the many homeless people who live on the streets of San Francisco. As I give you reporter Naomi Marcus's description of him, try to picture him in your mind, and think about whether or not you have seen him or someone like him recently. "Joseph Charles Moose is feeling all right this January morning. He has a bottle of Night Train wine in a paper bag on his lap, and he just had a good night's sleep in the boiler room under an Italian bakery near San Francisco's Fisherman's Wharf. He is holding a transistor radio and humming along, waving to friends from his perch on top of a park bench."

Have you seen him before? Or someone like him? Chances are you have. And chances are that you are all familiar with the topic of our presentation today: the problem of homelessness in the U.S. My classmates Mohammed, Carlos, and Vivian and I hope that by the end of our presentation you will be a bit more familiar with this problem. In our talk today we will cover the increasing number of homeless people, the four causes of homelessness, the public's attitudes toward homelessness, and solutions to the problem. I'll begin by giving you some startling statistics about the number of homeless people in the U.S. today.

b. Good morning, class. My name is Charles and these are my classmates Juan, Fatmah, and Tetsuo. Today we're going to talk to you about the homeless. I'll talk about how the numbers of homeless are rapidly increasing. Juan will tell you about the four causes of homelessness. Fatmah will describe the different attitudes that people have toward the homeless. And finally Tetsuo will talk about possible solutions to this problem and give our conclusion. Let me begin by telling you some statistics about how many homeless there are in the U.S.

c. Good afternoon, class. I'm Ahmed and these are my classmates Juanita and Kim. If you're like us, you've probably had direct experience with the problem that we'll be talking about today: the homeless people in America. Let me just take a quick poll. How many of you have given some spare change to homeless people you see on our city's streets? Hmmm. Quite a few, I see. And how many of you are slightly nervous when you see homeless people on the sidewalk and go across the street to avoid them? Yes, quite a few. If some of you raised your hands in agreement with one of these questions, then you're like our group: we give money to the homeless but we're uncomfortable around them. As part of our report today, we will let you know about the attitudes that other people in this country have about the homeless and you can compare yours with theirs. We'll also talk about some reasons for homelessness and some possible solutions. But first I'd like to give you some information about just how many homeless there are in the country and about the rapid increase in numbers of the homeless.

In addition to your opening and closing, you need to plan transitions between speakers. Here is an example of the closing and opening parts of a presentation by a three-member group speaking on homelessness. What techniques do they use to close their portion of the presentation? To begin their portion?

SPEAKER A (KUMIKO):
Now that I have reviewed for you some statistics to show that homelessness in the U.S. is indeed a serious problem and growing more serious every year, I'd like to introduce David, who will give you some information about why these numbers are growing.

SPEAKER B (DAVID):
Thank you. As Kumiko has pointed out, the statistics about homelessness are indeed shocking. And we all have probably wondered why there are so many homeless on the streets. In the next few minutes, I'd like to tell you what we discovered about the causes of homelessness and this increase in numbers. . . . Now that I have reviewed the four major causes of homelessness, our third member, Jaime, will fill us in on what we learned about attitudes toward the homeless and possible solutions to the problem. Jaime?

SPEAKER C (JAIME):
Thanks, David. Now in the last part of our presentation, I'll first report some rather surprising news about attitudes toward the homeless. At least our group found it surprising and we think you will too. First of all . . .

Activity 9:   Evaluating Transitions

Look at the following excerpts from other group presentations. Decide which transitions among speakers are effective and which could be better. How could you improve the weaker ones?

a. **SPEAKER A:**   As Jose mentioned before, the numbers of homeless are increasing every day. But why? Well, we discovered there are four main reasons for homelessness that are causing this increase. . . . That's it. Nita?

   SPEAKER B: Thank you, Suzie. I'd like to talk about another thing. That is, what attitudes people have toward the homeless. . . .

b. **SPEAKER A:**   Thank you, Ali. Now that Ali has given us some statistics on the number of homeless people in the U.S., I'd like to tell you about the reasons these folks are homeless. . . . So now that you've heard the four main reasons for homelessness, you're ready to hear about some possible solutions. Ivan will present these to you. Ivan?

   SPEAKER B: Thanks. As Irina has implied, we need to understand the causes of homelessness to consider possible solutions and evaluate their effectiveness. Let's consider the first cause—lack of affordable housing—and a possible solution.

c. **SPEAKER A:**   So as you can see, there are a great number of homeless people in the U.S. and the numbers are increasing every day. These numbers are one important point. The next point, my classmate Emilios will talk about.

   SPEAKER B: The second thing we want to talk about is the causes of homelessness. . . . And the third point will be presented by my classmate Kim.

Make information accessible and interesting to your audience. This group speaking on recycling uses posters and recyclable objects and has strong delivery skills.

PREPARING TO RESPOND TO QUESTIONS

At the end of a presentation, the audience may want to ask you questions, so you need to plan for this question-and-answer period. In a group presentation, one member can be designated to act as moderator. The moderator calls on members of the audience, repeats their questions for the audience, and then lets a group member respond. Sometimes the person in the audience may direct the question to a specific group member. If not, the moderator should select a group member to respond. The moderator can also keep the question-and-answer portion moving along by deciding when an answer or discussion has been sufficient and calling for the next question. Another way to handle the questions is for group members to simply take turns calling on audience members and answering their questions.

However the procedure is set up, several people in the audience should get a chance to ask questions, and all group members should have a chance to respond. Most audience members are annoyed when a question-and-answer period becomes a dialog between one member of the audience and one member of the group.

Individual and group presenters often prepare for the question-and-answer period by predicting questions the audience might ask and thinking of ways to answer them. Of course, presenters can't be expected to answer every question that the audience might come up with, but they should have a basic strategy for responding.

PREPARING YOUR NOTES AND VISUAL AIDS

Remember that unless you are giving a formal lecture on a highly technical subject, it is not a good idea to read a presentation. Note cards or a simple outline are preferable. In either case, use words and phrases to serve as a memory aid, and complete sentences only when you have a direct quotation. Speaking from notes forces you to use spoken English rather than written English; it improves your ability to maintain eye contact with your audience; and it makes your speech more spontaneous. For all these reasons, speaking from notes rather than reading from text improves communication with the audience and thus their interest in what you have to say.

For an informative presentation, it is especially effective to use visual aids such as charts, pictures, posters, and the chalkboard. These aids will make the information easier to understand and remember; they will keep your audience interested as well. For example, in a speech on homelessness, speakers could use an overhead projector or the chalkboard to list the four major causes of homelessness. Also, the group could prepare large charts and graphs like those in the source articles to help the audience understand these four causes. Some pictures of homeless people would also be effective attention-getters in an introduction or when reviewing the types of homeless people.

Some groups like to put the main divisions of their presentation on the board before they begin speaking; this gives the audience the overall plan of the presentation. If you aren't sure what visual aids you would like to include in this presentation, review the suggestions (and the cautions) in Unit 3 beginning on page 98 for using visual aids.

Activity 10:   Preparing Note Cards and Visual Aids

A.   Look at the speech excerpt in Activity 5. Prepare note cards that would be appropriate for this material. Remember not to put too much information on the cards. Two students can transfer the information on their cards to the board, and the class can critique the amount of information on each card and the actual wording of the notes.

B.   Discuss visual aids that would be appropriate for this segment of the talk.

PRACTICING AND EVALUATING THE PRESENTATIONS

You will probably want to rehearse your presentation several times, by yourself and with your group. As you practice, pay attention to the two sets of evaluation criteria that have been designed for this presentation: one is an individual evaluation and one is for the group. (See the evaluation forms at the end of the unit.)

Activity 11:   Reporting on Discussions and Presentations

Prepare a report on your reactions to the following:

A.   *Your group's discussions:* Here are some questions to help you reflect on your discussions. You don't need to answer all of them—they are only suggestions.

1. How well did your group adhere to the principles of small-group discussion. For example, did everyone get a chance to participate? Did some students dominate the discussions? If so, what could you have done about this? How did others in the group respond to those who talked too much? Why do you think they talked so much? Could you tell which members were clearly prepared for the discussions? How could you tell? Was the atmosphere cooperative? What made it so? If it wasn't, why not? Was there open agreement? Disagreement? Did you feel comfortable expressing your ideas and experiences? Did you have trouble understanding other group members? Did they seem to have trouble understanding you? Did group members ask for clarification?

2. Was the content of your discussions interesting? Why or why not? What could have made it more interesting?

3. What went well in the planning of your presentation? What problems, if any, did your group have in planning the presentation? Can you see any way to avoid such problems in the future? Think about how your presentation actually went. Were there problems in the presentation that could have been avoided by more careful planning? What were they, and how could they have been avoided?

B.   *Another group's presentation:* During another group's presentation, take careful notes on the content of the speech and fill out a group evaluation form. Then do the following:

1. Identify which presentation you are evaluating, and give an overview of the main points of the presentation.

2. Tell about the best features of the presentation in terms of content and organization. Comment on speech delivery if you wish.

3. Sum up your impressions of the presentation, including your reactions to the information presented.

Unit 4   Group Informative Presentation: Individual Evaluation

Speaker _____

Evaluator _____

Topic _____

RATING SYSTEM: + = excellent
                 √ = average
                 − = weak

Content/Organization/Preparation

_____ Main points were clear.

_____ Points had good supporting detail.

_____ Information was presented in the speaker's own words.

_____ Transitions from previous speaker and to next speaker were smooth.

_____ Content fit time limit.

_____ Responses to questions were clear.

Presentation/Delivery

_____ Eye contact

_____ Vitality

_____ Rapport with audience

_____ Use of note cards or outline

VOICE CONTROL:

_____ Volume

_____ Rate

_____ Fluency

_____ Comprehensibility

Comments and suggestions for improvement:

Unit 4   Group Informative Presentation: Group Evaluation

Group _____

Evaluator _____

Topic _____

RATING SYSTEM: + = excellent
√ = average
− = weak

_____ Introduction was effective.

_____ Main points were clear.

_____ Points had good supporting detail.

_____ Transitions between speakers were smooth.

_____ Conclusion was effective.

_____ Visual aids were effective.

_____ Presentation was well balanced among speakers.

_____ Presentation was interesting.

_____ Questions were answered clearly.

_____ Participation was approximately equal in the question-and-answer period.

_____ Question-and-answer period ran smoothly.

Main points of the presentation:

Comments:

Unit 5

Persuading Others: Solving a Problem

Diane and Jose are having a cup of coffee between classes. Diane brings up a problem she has at work.

JOSE: You look kind of tired, Diane. Did you stay up late last night studying for an exam or something?

DIANE: Well, not really, but I'm having some problems at work these days and it's really interfering with my ability to get my schoolwork done.

JOSE: Oh, yeah? That's too bad. What's going on?

DIANE: Well, it's a couple of people I work with. I'm really their supervisor in the office, but they seem to resent my authority.

JOSE: Hmm. Are they openly hostile, or what?

DIANE: It's more subtle than that. I'll give you an example. When I got to the office yesterday at noon, I found out that Cynthia, one of my problems, hadn't finished typing the report I needed for a meeting at 1:00 with my boss. I panicked and yelled at her and accused her of deliberately not doing the work to make me look bad.

JOSE: I don't blame you for being upset. What did she say?

DIANE: She said she was just doing the best she could and simply hadn't had time to do the typing. But I knew that wasn't true. I'd given her the report in plenty of time. She's

	really fond of taking long coffee breaks, and she's always talking on the phone to her boyfriend.
JOSE:	It sounds like she's basically lazy and incompetent. Is that it?
DIANE:	Oh, I don't know. She's bright enough. Maybe I'm just sort of angry that she doesn't take her work seriously.
JOSE:	Hmm. And the other person? You said there were two people giving you trouble.
DIANE:	Well, the other one is sort of the opposite. Ron also does work for me—and does it on time—but I have the feeling he's trying to get my job. He's always flattering my boss and making sure she knows how much work he's doing. I feel like he's really competing with me.
JOSE:	Hmm. That is a difficult situation. But, you know, Diane, I used to have similar problems in my job until I found a way to improve my relations with the people I worked with.
DIANE:	What did you do? Quit?
JOSE:	No, believe it or not, I took a psychology course called "Conflict Resolution" and started applying some of the stuff I learned in the class.
DIANE:	A psych course? I'm a business major, not a psychology major.
JOSE:	That doesn't matter. It's a really great course that helps you analyze conflict and see ways of dealing with it. Part of the course covers problems exactly like yours.
DIANE:	Oh, yeah? Well, since you've taken the course, maybe you can just tell me how I can get some of my conflicts at work resolved.
JOSE:	Sure, I can give you a couple of tips, but it's going to take more time than we've got now. Anyway, I still think you'd really like the course.
DIANE:	Maybe. But how come you had problems on the job? You don't look like the kind of person that has a lot of trouble relating to people.

JOSE: Oh, come on. We've all got conflicts: in our love life, with our parents, with the people we work with. And then there are the horrible problems of international conflicts. There we're not just talking about unhappiness on the job but about wars and death!

DIANE: You're right. Probably everyone could profit from a course like that. Maybe I could look at your notes some time. But in the meantime, could we get together this weekend to discuss those tips for dealing with Cynthia and Ron?

For Discussion

1. What do you think about Jose's solution to the problem Diane brings up?

2. Do you think Diane will take the course? Why or why not?

3. Do you agree with Jose's comment about the extent of the problem of conflict—on the personal, professional, and global level? Can you think of other areas of conflict that he has not mentioned?

4. Can you think of an example of a conflict that you have recently encountered? Have you resolved it? If so, did you have help in resolving it? From whom?

5. In the dialog, can you see any evidence of "conflict resolution" techniques that Jose uses with Diane?

SOLVING A PROBLEM

The introductory dialog exemplifies a kind of oral communication that is common in our everyday life: persuading others to take some course of action. Jose sees that Diane isn't successful in resolving conflicts she has with co-workers, so he gives her information about an option available to her—taking a psychology course. He also tries to convince her that it would be a good idea to do so; that is, he tries to persuade her that this is an appropriate course of action. The speech assignment for this unit will give you practice in persuading others that you have an effective solution to an important problem.

Like Jose, all of you regularly notice problems that need to be resolved. You even ask why people don't do something about them. For example, you may notice that it is very dark as you walk to the bus stop after class at night and wonder why there isn't better lighting or even an escort service on campus. Perhaps you are concerned about the environment and don't see any recycling bins for glass or aluminum at school or at your workplace. Most people just grumble about situations like these, but if you really want to change them, you have to come up with a plan of action. Sometimes there are opportunities to present plans of action, such as at a business meeting, at a student organization meeting, or at a public meeting like a city council hearing. This speech assignment gives you the opportunity to prepare and deliver a proposal in which you present a solution to a problem.

ASSIGNMENT: GIVING A PROBLEM/SOLUTION SPEECH

To complete this assignment, you need to do the following:

1. Think of a problem you have observed or encountered at school, at home, on the job, or in public.

2. Prepare a five- to six-minute speech in which you argue for a course of action to resolve the problem. For your speech, do the following:

   a. Describe the problem.

   b. Propose and describe a good solution.

   c. Counter arguments against this solution.

   d. Give reasons why your solution is preferable to other solutions.

3. Draw on outside sources—articles, books, pamphlets, interviews, and so on—as sources of facts and opinions for this speech.

CHOOSING APPROPRIATE PROBLEMS

The problem you select should interest not only you but the class as well. It should not be a problem that you alone face. A good way to come up with a problem of interest is to brainstorm for some problems that concern you and then organize your ideas into categories. For example, here is a list of some problems that might serve as the basis for this speech assignment.

PROBLEMS AT SCHOOL

too few available computer labs

library hours too short

too many general ed courses

recreational facilities crowded

insufficient number of tutors

PROBLEMS IN THE CITY

homeless on the streets

vandalism on public transportation

insufficient emergency medical care

car theft

PROBLEMS RELATED TO WORK

little information about part-time jobs

weak oral communication in job interviews

coping with work and school

racial discrimination in hiring/promotion

GENERAL PROBLEMS

violence on TV and in movies

ethics of politicians

drunk drivers

poor nutrition

Next, you need to decide which problems would be of interest to most members of your audience. For example, those problems related to school and city and the general problems would probably concern your classmates as well. In contrast, if very few people in your audience are currently working and lack work experience, then work-related problems might not be shared by classmates and would therefore not interest them.

The next step, thinking of a solution to the problem, will be easier for some problems than for others. Can you think of a solution to the problem of vandalism on public transportation? Maybe that is difficult for you. Perhaps someone who has worked for an ambulance service knows a good solution to the problem of insufficient emergency medical care, but most of us would have a hard time with that problem. Finally, even though you may find a problem that is of interest to everyone and you can come up with a solution you like, your problem and solution may be too complex to discuss in the time available to you for this speech. Here are two guidelines to help you choose an appropriate problem:

1. **Be careful not to choose too large a problem.** For example, though the threat of nuclear war is indeed an important and frightening problem, a solution that calls for abolishing all nuclear weapons simply cannot be discussed thoroughly in the time you have available.

Think of a problem that is familiar to you.

2. **Be careful that your solution clearly represents a specific course of action.** This course of action should be enforceable—that is, there should be an official way to make the change. For example, if you are discussing the problem of automobile deaths caused by drunk drivers, the solution "people who drink shouldn't drive" is a general principle, not a course of action. The choice of whether to drive after drinking is left up to individuals. A course of action in this case might be that the state law be changed, increasing the penalty for drunk driving to automatic loss of license on the first offense. The enforcement here is the stricter law.

In this example regarding drunk drivers, a single course of action—enacting a new state law—was proposed as the solution. However, it is possible for the solution to a problem to include several courses of action. For example, the problem of overcrowded school recreational facilities might be solved by these actions: (1) allocate certain hours at the facilities to certain groups of students, (2) rent the facilities of a nearby school to provide additional facilities, and (3) build more recreational facilities. Here, the solution consists of both immediate and long-range actions: the first action could be implemented immediately, the second action could be implemented in the near future, and the third action would have to be implemented in the more distant future. But the solution could also feature several courses of action that would be implemented simultaneously. For example, to solve the problem of insufficient tutors, a solution could include these actions: (1) actively recruit tutors through school organizations, (2) offer students units of academic credit for tutoring, and (3) set up private tutoring centers where students pay tutors directly. These three actions could be taken immediately.

Activity 1: Evaluating Possible Problems and Solutions

Consider each of the following problems and solutions, and decide which ones might be the basis of a good speech. Consider the appeal of the problem, the nature of the solution, and the time limit. Be prepared to explain your decisions.

a. **PROBLEM:** The traffic accident rate for teenage drivers is very high.

   SOLUTION: The state law should be changed, raising the minimum age for a driver's license to twenty-one.

b. **PROBLEM:** Resources are scarce.

   SOLUTION: This school should have a recycling program.

c. **PROBLEM:** People in this city are in danger of being assaulted.

   SOLUTION: Everyone should learn self-defense.

   The police force should be expanded.

d. **PROBLEM:** The city and the school have insufficient day-care facilities.

   SOLUTION: State restrictions on day-care facilities should be eased so that more people can operate centers.

e. **PROBLEM:** Because of budget cuts, the city's schools have large class sizes and students get little individual attention.

SOLUTION: University students should be required to take a one-semester course in which they work in the public schools helping students.

School volunteers can be recruited from senior citizens' groups.

f. PROBLEM: Recreational facilities at this school are very crowded.

SOLUTION: Students wishing to use the facilities should pay a small fee so that supervisors can be hired and facilities can stay open longer.

g. PROBLEM: Traffic on city streets and surrounding freeways is extremely congested, making it impossible for me to get to work on time.

SOLUTION: My employer should offer flexible hours for all employees.

Activity 2:   Evaluating Your Own Problems and Solutions

Brainstorm your own list of problems and possible solutions. Select two or three problems that could each serve as the focus for this speech. Write them out for evaluation by your classmates, using the problem/solution format in Activity 1. When evaluating one another's problems, consider these points:

1. Is the problem of interest to the audience?

2. Does the solution suggest a specific course of action? If the solution includes several courses of action, do they all seem equally effective?

3. Can the problem and solution be covered in the allotted time?

GATHERING INFORMATION FOR YOUR PRESENTATION

One of the keys to being persuasive is to be knowledgeable about your topic. Once you have decided on a problem and a solution for your presentation, you will need to have sufficient information to convince your audience that

What's the problem here? A difficult relationship? You'll need to find information about the problem you've chosen for this presentation.

you are well informed. You may need to gather information for at least four purposes:

- to show that the problem is indeed a problem
- to describe the solution in some detail
- to demonstrate difficulties with alternate solutions or to show potential consequences if no action is taken
- to document benefits of your solution

As with previous speech assignments, you can use library resources—books, magazines, pamphlets, films—as sources of information. You can also interview people who know about the problem and about the feasibility of the solution. This latter resource will be especially beneficial if you are speaking about a local problem, such as one on campus or in your city. You can also consider interviewing your classmates to get information on their attitudes toward your proposal.

A good way to begin is to think of questions you need answered and possible sources of information for those answers. For example, you might want to address a problem like the one mentioned in the dialog—difficulties in dealing with others, on the job or in any relationship—and want to propose a solution such as the one Jose offers: taking a course in conflict resolution. Your initial conceptualization of the problem/solution might look like this:

PROBLEM:

Nearly all students have problems in their interpersonal relationships that they could handle better. In addition, many students have a very minimal understanding of conflicts on a global level.

SOLUTION:

All students in this school should take a course in conflict resolution as one of their degree requirements.

Here are some questions that you might come up with:

1. Does this campus have a course (or courses) in conflict resolution?

   If so, what department is it in?

   What is the content of the course?

   Who takes this course?

   Why do they take it?

   Are there prerequisite courses?

2. What are the general degree requirements for all students?

   Is there a way this course could fit into those requirements?

   If so, what would be the procedure for getting this approved?

   If not, how could it be made part of the requirements?

   Who has the authority to decide on these requirements?

3. What are some benefits of this solution?

Activity 3:   Determining Information Needs and Sources of Information

A.   Using the preceding problem/solution example about a course in conflict resolution, do the following:

1. Think of questions in addition to those previously listed that you would want answered.

2. Look over all the questions and talk about sources of information to get answers to those questions. For example, what written sources could you use? If you plan to interview people, whom would you interview?

B.   Write out the problem and solution that you plan to use for this speech. Prepare a list of questions to get the information you need about your topic, and then list possible sources of information. Working in small groups, present this information to your group. The group can discuss the following:

1. What other questions are of interest? What else would audience members like to know? Are any of the questions not relevant?

2. What additional sources of information may be helpful?

ORGANIZING THE BODY OF YOUR SPEECH

As you gather information relevant to the problem and solution you will present, you need to think about how you can organize your ideas for this speech. Among the several possible methods of organization for a problem/solution speech, we suggest you use the following four-part one:

I. State and describe the problem

II. State and describe the solution

III. Counter arguments against this solution

IV. Show why this solution is desirable

    A. Note problems with other solutions

    B. State benefits of the solution

Let's consider each of these parts in more detail.

Stating and Describing the Problem

The first element is a clear statement of the problem. You also need to consider what or who has caused the problem and how serious it is. For example, for the proposal that all students take a course in conflict resolution, the problem might be stated this way:

> Because we are social beings, all of us face occasional conflicts in our interpersonal relationships—our relationships with friends, family members, fellow workers, teachers, and strangers we meet in daily life. We often do not know how to handle these conflicts effectively, and this can result in a range of bad feelings from minor irritation to extreme rage.

Here, the speaker is identifying a partial source of the problem (we are social beings) and stating the problem: our inability to handle conflict can result in a range of problems for us and for society. To find relevant information, the speaker might have consulted almanacs and statistical yearbooks, as well as professionals in the field and magazine and newspaper articles. In the description of the problem, the speaker might include information such as the following to convince the audience of the existence and severity of the problem:

- dramatic statistics on divorce as well as on child abuse and murder by family members

- statistics on the number of people who see psychologists, counselors, and psychotherapists

- information about companies' special training sessions for better working relationships and about their formal grievance procedures

- personal narratives of interpersonal conflicts (such as Diane's story, a family conflict, or a conflict in a romantic relationship)

- examples of diplomatic failure on the international level

- summary statistics gathered from classmates on typical conflicts in their lives

- statistics and a quotation from the director of the school counseling service about the number of students who seek help and the kinds of problems they face

- a quotation from a psychology professor who teaches a course in conflict resolution about why the course was started

Can you think of information that might be appropriate here?

Stating and Describing the Solution

The second element of your speech is a clear statement and description of the solution. For example, for the conflict resolution proposal, the statement might go like this:

> In view of the widespread and serious nature of this problem, I would like to propose the following solution: all students in this school should take a course in conflict resolution as one of their degree requirements.

Then the description of the solution might include information such as the following:

- what existing courses would meet this requirement
- what the contents of these courses are
- how many units of credit these courses offer
- how the requirement would fit in the general studies categories
- what course or requirement might be eliminated to add this course
- what restrictions, if any, would apply on when the course is to be taken
- what administrative procedures would be needed to implement this solution

What other information might be important in the description?

Activity 4:   Evaluating Classmates' Problems and Solutions

Plan and prepare in note form the first two parts of your speech: the statement and description of the problem and the statement and description of your proposed solution. Your notes can be on note cards or in an outline. In small groups or pairs, listen to and evaluate these two parts of one another's speeches. You may use these guidelines for evaluation:

1. Is the problem clear? Restate it in your own words.

2. Are you convinced that the problem is a serious one? If not, what sorts of information might convince you?

3. Is the solution clear? Is it a single course of action or does it have several parts? Restate the solution in your own words.

4. Is there sufficient description of the solution? If not, what more do you want to know about it?

Countering Arguments against the Solution

Generally, when people first hear a proposed solution to a problem, they immediately think of reasons why it is a bad idea. For example, here are some possible objections to the proposal for a required conflict resolution course:

> There are already too many requirements. Another course means more time and money.
>
> This course isn't relevant to my career in computer science.
>
> You can't prevent murder, divorce, and job conflict with a single course. This is an overly simplistic solution.

What other objections can you think of?

Part of the process of persuading your audience is to show them that you too have thought of objections to your solution but that you have a way to respond to them. To "counter" arguments means to show how they are invalid or inappropriate. It means to give arguments against the potential disadvantages of your solution. You need to first state the disadvantages (the objections) and then explain why these objections are unimportant or can be addressed in some other way. For example, in the conflict resolution speech, the speaker could deal with the first two objections in this way:

> Some of you may object to my proposal for a required course in conflict resolution by saying that you do not want any additional requirements for graduation. I would like to point out that what I am arguing for is *not* an additional requirement, but a substitution of this course for any one of the general studies requirements in the social sciences. Thus, you would take this course *in place of* a course in anthropology, history, social science, speech, or psychology. In this way, we students would have a course that is directly relevant to our lives instead of a course that seems unrelated to our lives or academic programs.

People are quick to find reasons why a proposed
solution to a problem won't work.

Another objection might be from students in fields such as computer science or biology. You might say that this course has no
relevance to your future careers because you will do highly technical work and are unlikely to work with others. Well, even if you
never work with others and spend your entire workday at a work-
station bent over your terminal, what about the rest of your life?
Don't you plan to be husbands or wives? Won't you have children? If not, even a single person has to shop, go out to dinner,
and visit with friends. And as I've said before, we are social ani-
mals, and therefore our ideas, needs, and desires will regularly
conflict with those of other people.

In these examples, the speaker expresses each point in this way:

STATE THE OBJECTION: Some of you may object to my proposal by
saying that . . .

COUNTER THE OBJECTION:	I would like to point out that . . .
STATE THE OBJECTION:	Another objection might be from students. . . . You might say that . . .
COUNTER THE OBJECTION:	Well, even if you . . . , what about . . . ? As I've said before, . . .

Activity 5:   Giving Objections and Countering Arguments

A.   Discuss how the speaker arguing for a course in conflict resolution could counter the third objection to the solution (the objection that this is an oversimplified solution to a large problem). Then in pairs or small groups, write out the actual statement of the objection and the countering of the objection that could be used in the speech. (Your statements can be similar to those written out for the first two objections in the preceding section, "Countering Arguments against the Solution.") The class can then evaluate these statements, paying attention to the language as well as the argument.

B.   In small groups, work on your own speech topics for this assignment. Each member should briefly describe his or her problem and solution, and other members should come up with two or three objections. The speaker should write them down. Then the group can discuss possible counter arguments to these objections. Follow this same procedure for each member's problem and solution.

Showing Why Your Solution Is Desirable

To persuade the audience of the value of your proposed solution, it is not enough for them to know what the solution is and why arguments against it are not convincing. They must also know how this course of action can benefit them. So, in this section of the speech, you need to state explicitly why your solution is desirable.

For some proposals, it might be appropriate to begin by reviewing other possible solutions and why they are problematic. For example, in the conflict resolution requirement speech, two alternate solutions might be:

- make the conflict resolution course an elective part of the curriculum

- provide students with conflict resolution information through a series of workshops run by the school counseling center

You could point out that the first alternate solution represents no change from the current situation: the course is already available as an elective. Thus, this solution does not respond to the fundamental belief that every college graduate, as an educated member of society, needs to know principles of conflict resolution. And for the second alternative solution, you could point out that such a program would require additional outside funding and would be subject to discontinuation; when budget troubles occur in a school, it is generally the special programs such as counseling and extra workshops that are the first to be cut.

Whether or not you mention flaws with other solutions, you need to describe the benefits of your solution. Here you can provide evidence that will move your audience to agree with you. Of course, you will have to explain each benefit to some degree, not simply list them. The benefits could be explained and supported with additional information such as statistics, authoritative opinions, narratives, and so on.

For example, for the proposal of a required course in conflict resolution, you might cite these benefits:

- Readings in the course will help students understand the related concepts of conflict, competition, and cooperation in human affairs. This background can facilitate understanding of human relationships in a variety of settings.

- The course will enable students to understand the factors that cause conflict and additionally to see how conflict is prolonged or resolved. Awareness of these factors, and the ability to analyze what is happening, represents the first step toward more effective relationships.

- The course will make students aware of the role of communication in conflict resolution and will enable them to develop skills of conflict management and resolution as well as to develop new leadership skills.

- Students from other cultures can gain new insights into American culture through the readings and activities in the course.

Activity 6:   Stating and Evaluating Benefits

In small groups, discuss the benefits of the solutions you are going to propose for this speech assignment. Each member should briefly state his or her problem and solution and then tell the group about benefits of the solution. Group members can then evaluate the benefits and perhaps suggest others.

Outlining the Body of Your Speech

Once you have worked out the four main parts of your problem/solution speech, you need to combine them and prepare a complete outline. The following sample outline shows how we might organize the body of the conflict resolution speech according to the four-component process: (1) statement of the problem, (2) statement of the solution, (3) countering arguments against the solution, and (4) reasons why the solution is desirable.

I. Problem
   A. Difficulties in interpersonal relationships
      1. e.g., best friend—problems at work
      2. e.g., brother—broke up with girlfriend
      3. e.g., cousin—fights with parents
      4. e.g., me—problems with landlord
      5. source: conflicting values, perceptions, lack of communication—led to escalation, not resolution
   B. Concerns about future of planet
      1. global misunderstandings and conflict—e.g., Gulf War
      2. lack of knowledge of cultural values, norms, lack of empathy—e.g., U.N. Security Council
   C. Statement of problem: ignorance of the nature of conflict and ways of responding at personal through global level
II. Solution: Required course in conflict resolution
   A. Description of course
      1. Availability
         a. Offered in two departments: psychology and speech
         b. Given every semester, occasionally in summer

      c. No prerequisite

      d. Upper-division course—for juniors and seniors

  2. Content

      a. Speech course—4 units

         1) conflict theories—Marx, Simmel, Rapoport, etc.

         2) role of communication in conflict

         3) research on conflict, especially gaming and simulation

         4) conflict resolution and management skills

         5) application to interpersonal and intergroup conflict

      b. Psychology course—3 units

         1) theory and application: conflict at four levels—interpersonal, organizational, national, global

         2) includes unit on "waging peace"

 B. Fit with academic structure

  1. Could count in general studies program (3 of 40 units)

      a. Replacement for a social sciences course, not an addition

  2. Procedure for approval

      a. Petition to school General Studies Committee

      b. General Studies Committee approves

      c. Academic Senate must approve

  3. Would require additional sections

      a. Interviews: not a problem—departments have faculty

      b. Could be added in other departments—e.g., International Relations, Linguistics

III. Countering objections

 A. Argument: No more requirements

      Response: Not added, would replace another requirement—more meaningful than other course (history, anthropology, etc.)

 B. Argument: Not appropriate for technical majors

      Response: Everyone has social relations—family, etc.
                Everyone has stake in global survival

 C. Argument: Big problem, too small a solution

      Response: Need to begin somewhere; cost-effective solution; raising awareness, expand to others, can make a difference in daily lives

IV. Why solution is desirable

    A. Other solutions not good

        1. Make course elective
           But: Only students who don't need it would take it
               Seriousness of problem demands all take it

        2. Get information through other means—e.g., counseling workshops
           But: Can't get depth of a course this way (e.g., reading, papers)
               Financially a risk—could be cut easily

    B. Benefits of a course

        1. Gain understanding of conflict, competition, cooperation; human relations in variety of settings

        2. Learn factors that cause conflict and how it's prolonged, resolved; awareness, analysis give insights into better relationships

        3. See central role of communication; develop management and leadership skills

        4. Learn about American culture; attitudes, behaviors re conflict

---

Activity 7: Practicing Transitions

To practice using transitional expressions (review the discussion of transitions in Unit 3 beginning on page 81 if needed), refer to the sample outline and do the following:

1. Make up a rhetorical question to introduce part II-A.

2. Think of a sentence that could signal an end to part II and introduce part III.

3. Think of a sentence that could signal an end to part III and introduce part IV.

4. Think of a sentence that could link part IV-A to part IV-B.

Planning Visual Aids

Now that you have completed the outline of the body of your speech, think about visual aids that could make your speech especially persuasive. (Review the section on visual aids beginning on page 98.) The visual aids you choose could present information or they could serve to get the audience involved in the problem you are discussing. For the sample speech on conflict resolution, the speaker could present a diagram of current general education requirements showing how the change would fit, present a graph of rising divorce statistics, project several slides, or bring in photographs showing conflict or disagreement. Can you think of other visual aids that might be appropriate for this speech?

*Activity 8:   Evaluating Your Classmates' Outlines
                and Plans for Visual Aids*

Bring several copies of the completed outline of your speech to class. In small groups, review each group member's outline, focusing on its completeness. Also, review each group member's plan for visual aids to accompany the speech, giving suggestions where necessary.

PREPARING YOUR CONCLUSION

In the conclusion to an informative speech, you usually summarize or restate main ideas you want the audience to remember. In a persuasive speech, the conclusion is your final chance to convince your audience of the importance of your ideas and convert them to your point of view. Therefore, you don't want simply to summarize your main points. But what can you do to provide a strong ending that enlists your audience's support?

You can begin by restating the explicit focus of your speech. For example, in the sample speech, this would be the belief that all students will benefit from taking a course in conflict resolution and that they should follow the strategies you have suggested for making this solution a reality. You can then motivate the audience to participate in this solution by reminding them of the benefits of such an action or of the consequences of doing nothing. Finally, you need to bring the speech to a close in an effective manner. Here, you

In your conclusion, you can
restate the benefits of your proposal and
close with a dramatic statement or question.

might refer back to a rhetorical question, a story, or a dramatic statistic that you used earlier in your speech. Or you might close with a striking quotation or other dramatic statement.

Activity 9:   Evaluating Conclusions

Determine which of the following would be the most effective conclusion for the speech proposing a required course in conflict resolution. Give reasons for your choice. Use the following questions for evaluation if you wish:

1. Does the conclusion make the focus of the speech (that is, the solution that the speaker is arguing for) clear?

2. If appropriate, does the conclusion indicate what the audience is being asked to do?

3. Does the conclusion motivate the audience, either by stating the benefits of the solution or by pointing out the negative consequences of not taking action?

4. Does the conclusion have a strong closing?

5. What is especially good about the conclusion?

a. In conclusion, you can see that all of us have problems in our daily lives with interpersonal relationships and with understanding the nature of conflict. To get help with this, we can spend great sums of money on psychiatrists and counselors in order to learn to be better communicators with people around us. Or we can find a much cheaper and more intellectually stimulating solution: we can all take a course in this school that teaches us about conflict resolution. I hope you will join me in requesting this change. There's no time like the present to start making our relationships better!

b. As I have pointed out to you today, resolving conflicts in our daily lives is a problem we all face; it's a problem that nations face as well, and one that if not carefully handled can result in the destruction of our planet. I have suggested a simple remedy to this problem that can help those of us in the university community: that is, that all students must take a course in conflict resolution in order to graduate from this school. We can take a course in either the psychology department or the speech department, and this solution will give us certain benefits: we can learn more about the related ideas of conflict, competition, and cooperation in human affairs; we can understand factors that cause conflict; we can see how important communication is to helping us prolong or resolve conflict; and we can learn more about American culture. I think you can easily see how helpful such a course can be, and when you take this course you will agree with my friend Maria who said, "This course in conflict resolution was the best one I've taken at this school."

c. Today I have pointed out that there is a way that students in this school can avoid becoming counted in our country's shocking statistics on divorce and violence. How can this come about? We can get signatures on this petition to the general studies committee insisting on a required course in conflict resolution. By taking such a course, all of us will better understand what conflict, competition, and cooperation are all about. In the midst of conflict with friends, relatives, spouses, employers, or strangers, we will be able to analyze what is happening and be able to resolve the conflict rather than prolong it. With improved communication skills and understanding of American culture, we will be recognized as leaders in our jobs and in our communities. In short, by circulating this petition, we can do our part to create a more peaceful, compassionate world. As former Senator J. William Fulbright once said, "Only on the basis of an understanding of our behavior can we hope to control it in such a way as to ensure the survival of the human race."

Activity 10:   Evaluating Your Classmates' Conclusions

Prepare the conclusion to your speech in an outline or on note cards. Then in small groups, listen to and evaluate each conclusion. Listen more than once if necessary, and give suggestions for improvement as needed. You can use the questions in Activity 9 to guide your evaluation.

PREPARING YOUR INTRODUCTION

Just as with information speeches, you need to grab the audience's interest at the beginning of persuasive speeches. This can be accomplished through the use of statistics, humor, stories, quotations, and so on. (Review the section in Unit 3 on page 87 regarding these techniques.) Once you have your listeners' attention, you need to begin to build their confidence in you: you want to convince them that you know what you are talking about and that your ideas are worth taking seriously. In other words, you need to establish your credibility as a speaker. How can you do this?

You can prove to them that you are reliable and believable by showing that you are informed about your subject, whether through firsthand experience or through reading and interviewing. (Of course, you will want to do this throughout your speech, not just in the introduction.) In addition, you can establish credibility by letting your audience know why you are speaking on this subject. Your manner of delivery can aid your credibility as well: if you speak in a friendly, sincere, concerned fashion, you build good rapport; if you are self-assured and poised, you gain the audience's confidence in you and consequently your ideas.

As part of your introduction, you will probably want to state the general topic of the speech as a way to orient the audience. You may also wish to show why this topic is of interest or importance. Ordinarily, it is *not* appropriate to give an overview of the content of the persuasive speech as you may have done in your informative speech.

Activity 11: *Evaluating Introductions*

Decide which of the following would be the most effective introduction for a speech proposing a required course on conflict resolution. Give reasons for your decision. You can use these questions for evaluation:

1. How does the opening attract attention?

2. Does the introduction build rapport with the audience?

3. Is the topic of the speech made clear?

4. How does the speaker establish credibility?

5. What do you especially like about the introduction?

a. I'd like to begin today with some statistics. How many women do we have in this class? Sixteen? Okay. I'd like you eight women on this side of the room to raise your hands. You are the unlucky half: according to statistics provided by the Fund for the Feminist Majority, more than one half of all women in this country will be victims of sexual assault and/or domestic violence in their life-times. So you women could be the half that will suffer. Now here's another more well known statistic. How many of you are mar-ried? Only two? But most of you plan to marry, right? Now I'd like everyone on this side of the room to raise your hands. You represent the portion of the class whose marriages will end in divorce—that's over half the class. Well, you may say, "It won't happen to me," but today I'm going to propose a plan of action to you so you can be much more certain that it won't. I'm going to talk about a problem we all face: namely, dealing with conflict in our relationships with others.

b. I've written the word "conflict" on the board, and I want each of you to think about a conflict you've had recently—with your par-ents, with your boss, with your boyfriend or girlfriend, even perhaps with your English teacher. I work in the counseling center on campus, so I know from my peer counseling that students like us have many conflicts as we try to juggle the responsibilities of school, work, home, and family. I personally have conflicts with my parents over my social life—they want to control who I see and how much time I spend socializing, and I object to this control. But from my studies in psychology and my work in the counseling center, I have learned that there are ways to handle these conflicts effectively, to keep them from escalating out of control and resulting in bad feelings and ruined relationships. So today, I am going to propose a plan of action that can help all of you learn to deal with conflict and avoid having to come see us in the counseling center.

c. Let me tell you a brief story about something that recently happened to me and my roommate. A couple of weeks ago I had a lot of friends over for dinner on a Sunday night, and by the time they left, it was late and I was too tired to clean up the kitchen. And on Monday I have an early class so I had to leave the house without cleaning up. Well, when I got home that evening after a hard day at school, I found that my roommate had put all the dirty dishes and pots and pans on my bed with a note: "Here's your mess." Of course, that made me angry, and we hardly spoke to each other for a week. My point is that this kind of conflict can happen to any of us in our daily lives, but it doesn't have to go so far as putting dirty dishes on the bed and everyone being hurt and angry for a week. Today I'm going to tell you a solution I propose for helping us learn about ways to deal with conflict. I'm going to propose that we all take a course in conflict resolution and that this course should be required for graduation. I'll describe the content of the course and show how it can be implemented. Then I'll talk about some objections to such a course and why they are not valid. Finally, I'll tell you some benefits of the course, showing you why it is an excellent solution to a problem we all face.

Activity 12: *Evaluating Your Classmates' Introductions*

Prepare the introduction to your speech in an outline or on note cards and bring it to class. In small groups, listen to and evaluate each introduction. Listen more than once if necessary, and give suggestions for improvement as needed. You can use the questions in Activity 11 to aid your evaluation.

Speak with conviction. Ways of showing conviction depend on your individual style. Some speakers put a lot of energy into their voices and gestures; others speak in a quiet but intense manner.

DELIVERING AND EVALUATING PROBLEM/SOLUTION SPEECHES

In giving a persuasive speech, it is especially important that you speak with conviction—that is, as if you are 100 percent sure of the position you have taken and of the value of your ideas and evidence. According to Rudolph F. Verderber, an authority on speech communication, conviction can be shown in a variety of ways. For example, some speakers show conviction by their animation: they put a lot of energy into their voices and into their gestures. Other speakers show conviction by speaking in a quiet but intense manner. Since personal style determines the way we speak convincingly, our approaches will differ. The one certainty is that an audience can easily detect a lack of conviction.

In evaluating your classmates' speeches, you should pay special attention to whether the speech is convincing. The persuasiveness of the speech will depend on both the content and the conviction of the speaker. As the evaluation form at the end of the unit indicates, you should fill in the actual information for the content in addition to rating that content.

Activity 13:   *Reporting on a Problem/Solution Speech*

Choose a speech on a topic that you find interesting. While your classmate is speaking, take careful notes on the content of the speech, using the evaluation form at the end of the unit. Then prepare a report in which you do the following:

1. State the problem and solution clearly, summarizing your classmate's remarks about why the problem is important, what the solution entails, how objections can be countered, and why the solution is desirable.

2. Discuss what made the speech interesting and convincing (or not convincing), drawing on what you know about using information as well as good delivery techniques to promote speaker credibility.

Unit 5   Problem/Solution Speech

Speaker _____

Evaluator _____

Topic _____

RATING SYSTEM: + = excellent
                 √ = average
                 − = weak

Content/Organization/Preparation

Fill in the relevant information where spaces are provided.

_____ Introduction was appropriate.

_____ Problem was stated clearly:

_____ Problem was described adequately.

_____ Solution was stated clearly:

_____ Solution was described adequately.

_____ Arguments against the proposal were countered.

_____ Benefits of solution were clear.

_____ Speech had a suitable conclusion.

_____ Speaker answered questions well.

_____ Content fit time limit.

Presentation/Delivery

_____ Eye contact   _____ Rapport with audience

_____ Vitality   _____ Spoke convincingly

_____ Gestures   _____ Use of note cards or outline

                            _____ Effective use of visual aids

VOICE CONTROL:

_____ Volume

_____ Rate

_____ Fluency

_____ Comprehensibility

Overall

_____ The speech was convincing. Tell why or why not:

Other comments:

Unit 6

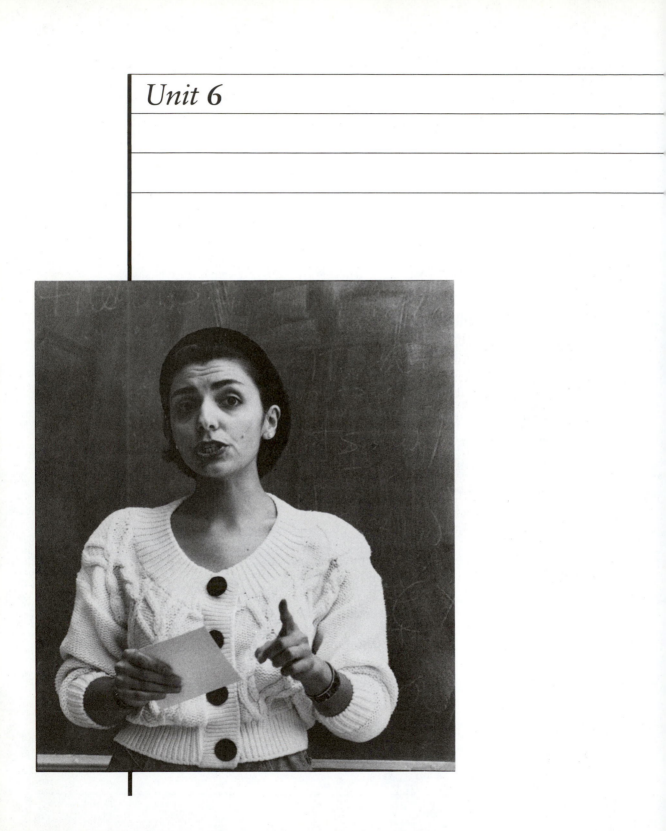

Persuading Others:
Taking a Position

RESOURCE ARTICLE

In the following article, the author discusses "English-only" sentiments in the United States.

ENGLISH ONLY

FROM ITS INCEPTION, THE UNITED STATES HAS BEEN A MULTILINGUAL NATION.

At the time of the nation's founding, it was commonplace to hear as many as 20 languages spoken in daily life, including Dutch, French, German and numerous Native American languages. Even the Articles of Confederation were printed in German, as well as English. During the 19th and early 20th centuries, the nation's linguistic diversity grew as successive waves of Europeans immigrated to these shores and U.S. territory expanded to include Puerto Rico, Hawaii and the Philippines.

Just as languages other than English have always been a part of our history and culture, debate over establishing a national language dates back to the country's beginnings. John Adams proposed to the Continental Congress in 1780 that an official academy be created to "purify, develop, and dictate usage of" English. His proposal was rejected as undemocratic and a threat to individual liberty.

Nonetheless, restrictive language laws have been enacted

Taken from American Civil Liberties Union Briefing Paper, Number 6. Reprinted by permission of the ACLU.

periodically since the late 19th century, usually in response to new waves of immigration. These laws, in practice if not in intent, have punished immigrants for their foreignness and violated their rights.

In the early 1980s, again during a period of concern about new immigration, a movement arose that seeks the establishment of English as the nation's official language. The "English Only" movement promotes the enactment of legislation that restricts or prohibits the use of languages other than English by government agencies and, in some cases, by private businesses. The movement has met with some success, "English Only" laws having been passed in several states. And, for the first time in the nation's history, an English Language Amendment to the Constitution has been proposed.

The ACLU opposes "English Only" laws because they can abridge the rights of individuals who are not proficient in English, and because they perpetuate false stereotypes of immigrants and non-English speakers. We believe, further, that such laws are contrary to the spirit of tolerance and diversity embodied in our Constitution. An English Language Amendment to the Constitution would transform that document from being a charter of liberties and individual freedom into a charter of restrictions that limits, rather than protects, individual rights.

Here are the ACLU's answers to some questions frequently asked by the public about "English Only" issues.

What is an
"English Only" law?

"English Only" laws vary. Some state statutes simply declare English as the "official" language of the state. Other state and local edicts limit or bar government's provision of non-English language assistance and services. For example, some restrict bilingual education programs, prohibit multilingual ballots, or forbid non-English government services in general—including such services as courtroom translation or multilingual emergency police lines.

Where have such laws been enacted?

Sixteen states have "English Only" laws and many others are considering such laws. In some states, the laws were passed decades ago during up-surges of nativism, but most were passed within the last few years. The "English Only" states are Arizona, Arkansas, California, Colorado, Florida, Georgia, Illinois, Indiana, Kentucky, Mississippi, Nebraska, North Carolina, North Dakota, South Carolina, Tennessee and Virginia.

What are the consequences of "English Only" laws?

Some versions of the proposed English Language Amendment would void almost all state and federal laws that require the government to provide services in languages other than English. The services affected would include: health, education and social welfare services; job training and translation assistance to crime victims and witnesses in court and administrative proceedings; voting assistance and ballots; drivers' licensing exams, and AIDS-prevention education.

Passage of an "English Only" ordinance by Florida's Dade County in 1980, barring public funding of activities that involved the use of languages other than English, resulted in the cancellation of all multi-cultural events and bilingual services, ranging from directional signs in the public transit system to medical services at the county hospital.

Where basic human needs are met by bilingual or multilingual services, the consequences of eliminating those services could be dire. For example, the *Washington Times* reported in 1987 that a 911 emergency dispatcher was able to save the life of a Salvadoran woman's baby son, who had stopped breathing, by coaching the mother in Spanish over the telephone to administer mouth-to-mouth and cardiopulmonary resuscitation until the paramedics arrived.

Do "English Only" laws affect only government services and programs?

"English Only" laws apply primarily to government programs. However, such laws can also affect private businesses. For example, several Southern California cities have passed ordinances that forbid or restrict the use of foreign languages on private business signs.

Some "English Only" advocates have opposed a telephone company's use of multilingual operators and multilingual directories, Federal Communications Commission licensing of Spanish-language radio stations, and bilingual menus at fast food restaurants.

Who is affected by "English Only" laws?

"English Only" campaigns target primarily Latinos and Asians, who make up the majority of recent immigrants. Most language minority residents are Spanish-speaking, a result of the sharp rise in immigration from Latin America during the mid-1960s.

While the overwhelming majority of U.S. residents—96 percent—are fluent in English, approximately ten million residents are not fluent, according to the most recent census.

How do "English Only" laws deprive people of their rights?

The ACLU believes that "English Only" laws are inconsistent with the Equal Protection Clause of the Fourteenth Amendment. For example, laws that have the effect of eliminating courtroom translation severely jeopardize the ability of people on trial to follow and comprehend the proceedings. "English Only" laws interfere with the right to vote by banning bilingual ballots, or with a child's right to education by restricting bilingual instruction. Such laws also interfere with the right of workers to be free of discrimination in workplaces where employers have imposed "speak English only" rules.

In 1987, the ACLU adopted a national policy opposing "English Only" laws or laws that would "characterize English as the official language in the United States . . . to the extent that [they] would mandate or encourage the erosion" of the rights of language minority persons.

What kinds of language policies were adopted with regard to past generations of immigrants?

Our nation was tolerant of linguistic diversity up until the late 1800s, when an influx of Eastern and Southern Europeans, as well as Asians, aroused nativist sentiments and prompted the enactment of restrictive language laws. A 1911 Federal Immigration Commission report falsely argued that the "old" Scandinavian and German immigrants had assimilated quickly, while the "new" Italian and Eastern European immigrants were inferior to their predecessors, less willing to learn English, and more prone to political subversion.

In order to "Americanize" the immigrants and exclude people thought to be of the lower classes and undesirable,

English literacy requirements were established for public employment, naturalization, immigration and suffrage. The New York State Constitution was amended to disfranchise over one million Yiddish-speaking citizens. The California Constitution was similarly amended to disfranchise Chinese, who were seen as a threat to the "purity of the ballot box."

Ironically, during the same period, the government sought to "Americanize" Native American Indian children by taking them from their families and forcing them to attend English-language boarding schools, where they were punished for speaking their indigenous languages.

The intense anti-German sentiment that accompanied the outbreak of World War I prompted several states, where bilingual schools had been commonplace, to enact extreme language laws. For example, Nebraska passed a law in 1919 prohibiting the use of any other language than English through the eighth grade. The Supreme Court subsequently declared the law an unconstitutional violation of due process.

Today, as in the past, "English Only" laws in the U.S. are founded on false stereotypes of immigrant groups. Such laws do not simply disparage the immi-

grants' native languages but assault the rights of the people who speak the languages.

Why are bilingual ballots needed since citizenship is required to vote, English literacy is required for citizenship, and political campaigns are largely conducted in English?

Naturalization for U.S. citizenship does not require English literacy for people over 50, and/or who have been in the U.S. for 20 years or more. Thus, there are many elderly immigrant citizens whose ability to read English is limited, and who cannot exercise their right to vote without bilingual ballots and other voter materials. Moreover, bilingual campaign materials and ballots foster a better informed electorate by increasing the information available to people who lack English proficiency.

Doesn't bilingual education slow immigrant children's learning of English, in contrast to the "sink or swim" method used in the past?

The primary purpose of bilingual programs in elementary and secondary schools, which use both English and a child's native language to teach all subjects, is to develop proficiency in English and, thus, facilitate the child's transition to all-English instruction. Although debate about this approach continues, the latest studies show that bilingual education definitely enhances a child's ability to acquire the second language. Some studies even show that the more extensive the native language instruction, the better students perform all around, and that the bilingual method engenders a positive self-image and self-respect by validating the child's native language and culture.

The "sink or swim" experience of past immigrants left more of them underwater than not. In 1911, the U.S. Immigration Service found that 77 percent of Italian, 60 percent of Russian, and 51 percent of German immigrant children were one or more grade levels behind in school compared to 28 percent of American-born white children. Moreover, those immigrants who did manage to "swim" unaided in the past, when agricultural and factory jobs were plentiful, might not do so well in today's "high-tech" economy, with its more rigorous educational requirements.

But won't "English Only" laws speed up the assimilation of today's immigrants into our society and prevent their isolation?

In fact, contrary to what "English Only" advocates assume, the vast majority of today's Asian and Latino immigrants are acquiring English proficiency and assimilating as fast as did earlier generations of Italian, Russian and German immigrants. For example, research studies show that over 95 percent of first generation Mexican Americans are English proficient, and that more than 50 percent of second generation Mexican Americans have lost their native tongue entirely.

In addition, census data reveal that nearly 90 percent of

Latinos five years old or older speak English in their households. And 98 percent of Latinos surveyed said they felt it is "essential" that their children learn to read and write English "perfectly." Unfortunately, not enough educational resources are available for immigrants—over 40,000 are on the waiting list for over-enrolled adult English classes in Los Angeles. "English Only" laws do not increase resources to meet these needs.

The best insurance against social isolation of those who immigrate to our nation is acceptance—and celebration—of the differences that exist within our ethnically diverse citizenry. The bond that unites our nation is not linguistic or ethnic homogeneity but a shared commitment to democracy, liberty and equality.

For Discussion

1. What is the point of view of the author toward English-only laws?

2. What are some of the arguments the author presents to support this point of view?

3. What supporting details do you think may appeal (1) to the emotions (that is, to people's feelings) and (2) to the intellect (that is, to people's sense of logic and ideas)?

4. What is your opinion of English-only laws?

5. What policies do countries that you have lived in or are familiar with have concerning use of an official language?

SPEAKING TO PERSUADE

We all persuade others to do things in daily life. For instance, you may want to persuade a friend or relative to drive you to school so that you don't have to take the bus. Or a classmate may need to convince the teacher that she will do a better job if she can give her speech during the next class period. Another student may have to persuade an interviewer that he is the right candidate for the job. Learning to use appropriate persuasive techniques can benefit you and can also help you see how others persuade you.

Your assignment for this unit is to give a persuasive speech. Persuasive speeches are, of course, common in many fields: in business, where salespersons have to convince others of the value of their products; in courts of law, where lawyers try to persuade the jury; in politics, where politicians solicit the support of the public. According to Rudolph F. Verderber, author of several books on public speaking, persuasive speeches are normally given for one of three purposes: (1) to reinforce a belief held by an audience, (2) to establish a belief, or (3) to change a belief held by an audience. An additional goal may be to move the audience to act. As you prepare your speech, keep these general purposes in mind.

ASSIGNMENT: GIVING A PERSUASIVE SPEECH

The assignment for this unit is a six- to seven-minute speech in which you attempt to convince your audience that your point of view is the one that they should endorse, adopt, and/or take action on. You will be expected to do outside research to gather information for this speech. You should prepare an outline and a list of references to turn in. In your speech, you need to do the following:

1. Provide any background information necessary for the audience to understand your speech.

2. Clearly express your point of view.

3. Give three or four clear arguments to support your point of view.

4. Provide convincing evidence to defend your arguments.

5. Respond to two or three important opposing arguments.

Choosing a Topic

For this assignment, choose a topic that you feel strongly about. A good place to start looking for a topic is in the list provided for the group presentations in Unit 4 beginning on page 111. For example, if you choose gun control as your topic, then you could take a position either in favor of or opposed to gun control; if you choose abortion, then you could take either a pro-choice or a pro-life position. In the article at the beginning of this unit, the authors took a position against English-only laws and an English language amendment to the Constitution. As you choose your topic, consider whether you will be able to present strong enough arguments to convince the audience of the validity of your position. If you think you will have difficulty defending your position, then you may need to look for another topic.

Analyzing Your Audience

The background, values, attitudes, and opinions of your audience are especially important when you are planning a persuasive speech. You need to know how they feel about your position on your topic. Audience members may agree or disagree with you, or they may have no opinion. People who have no opinion generally fit into one of three categories: (1) they don't know about the topic, (2) they are neutral—that is, neither pro nor con—or (3) they don't care. You will need to take these attitudes into account as you plan your speech and select your evidence.

One way to find out about your classmates' attitudes is to talk to them individually—that is, to conduct a survey. It is especially important that the survey questions be clear, so you will need to check the clarity of the questions before conducting your survey.

EXAMPLES

CLEAR QUESTION: Should the United States government pass a law making it illegal for private citizens to own handguns?

UNCLEAR QUESTION: What do you think about handguns?

CLEAR QUESTION: Do you think there should be an English-only amendment to the Constitution?

UNCLEAR QUESTION: Should everybody in the United States be required to speak English?

Activity 1:   *Doing a Survey to Determine Classmates' Attitudes*

Using a list of students in the class, circulate around the room and survey your classmates to find out their attitudes toward your position on your topic. Take notes on whether they agree, disagree, or have no opinion about it and, if possible, on some of the reasons for their points of view. For homework, summarize the results of your survey.

Be careful not to overuse expressions indicating that
you are giving an opinion.

EXPRESSING OPINIONS

The purpose of your persuasive speech is to convince your audience of the
validity of your opinion about your topic. In stating and supporting your arguments, you will be using additional opinions, both yours and those of
others. Whenever possible, these opinions should be based on facts. Therefore, you need to recognize the difference between a fact and an opinion. A
fact can be independently verified; an opinion, on the other hand, results from
conclusions you have drawn based on information available to you.

Activity 2:   Distinguishing between Facts and Opinions

Decide which of the following sentences are facts and which are opinions.

a. Everyone who lives in the United States should learn to speak English.

b. Sixteen states in the United States now have English language laws.

c. This amendment will stop a direct attack on our way of life.

d. In Los Angeles, 40,000 people are on the waiting list for adult English classes.

e. The English-only movement threatens the civil rights of millions of Americans.

Following are some expressions that you may use to express opinions:

I think/feel/believe	My point of view is
In my opinion/estimation/view	It seems to me that
From my point of view	As I see it

Note, however, that only one of these expressions should be used to indicate an opinion.

EXAMPLE OF OVERUSE: In my opinion, I think that people who favor English-only laws need to be educated more about this issue.

Usually, when you are speaking, it is quite clear that you are expressing an opinion and it is unnecessary to use such expressions. However, you may choose to use them occasionally for emphasis. Of course, if you are expressing an opinion taken from one of your sources, you must mention the name of the organization or person holding the opinion.

EXAMPLES:

According to the ACLU, English-only laws abridge the rights of individuals who are not proficient in English.

In Steve Nichols' opinion, English is not endangered by other languages, but can be enriched by them.

Activity 3:   Expressing an Opinion on Your Speech Topic

The following activity, in which each student gives a two-minute speech, can be done as a whole class or in small groups. To complete the activity, you need to do the following:

1. Write the topic on which you are planning to give your persuasive speech at the top of a note card. Then write down your opinion about the topic.

   EXAMPLE:

   English Language Amendment
   I believe that the U.S. government should not add an English language amendment to the Constitution.

2. Take five minutes to make the following preparations for your speech:

   a. Plan an opening in which you make clear the topic and your position.

   b. Plan the supporting arguments you will use to make your position convincing.

   c. Write down some key words that you can use during your talk.

   d. Think about some expressions of opinion you may wish to use.

3. Deliver your two-minute speech. A member of the class/group should then restate your position and summarize your supporting points for clarification. Finally, members of the class/group may ask you questions for a brief period of time.

PREPARING YOUR SPEECH

As you prepare your speech you will need to do several things: gather resource material, choose arguments to support your position, organize your arguments, choose supporting evidence, find ways to appeal to your audience, decide on appropriate transitions, and prepare a conclusion and an introduction.

Gathering Resource Material

For your persuasive speech, you will be required to use one or more written sources. If it is appropriate, you may, of course, also gather information from interviews. The more you know, the stronger your speech will be. You should be prepared to look for sources that provide background for your topic as well as for those that take a particular position. You will find that many articles do both, but the authors may have selected background information specifically to support their own position. Although the material that will be most useful to you will come from sources expressing the point of view that you hold, it is also important for you to consider sources expressing the opposing point of view. In order to give a balanced presentation, you need to acknowledge opposing arguments and do your best to counter them.

Usually, the most current information can be found in journal, magazine, and newspaper articles; books can be a good source of historical information. All of these are available to you in school and city libraries. The *Readers' Guide to Periodical Literature* is a good source for magazine articles, and most large libraries have computerized journal and newspaper indexes, too. In addition, pamphlets can be a good source of information. You can find them in your library's pamphlet file, or you can get them directly from organizations such as the AIDS Foundation, Amnesty International, or Greenpeace. Your reference librarian can help with addresses and telephone numbers for these organizations.

After you find some relevant sources, make copies and then mark the parts of the sources that contain evidence you think might be useful for your speech. In the English-only article, one could mark sections that include information about the following: the history of language laws, civil rights, government services, bilingual education, and the social effects of English-only laws.

Documenting Your Sources

For this assignment, you will be required to turn in a list of references with your speech outline; providing such information is what we mean by "documenting your sources." When presenting a speech at a conference or public meeting, a speaker normally includes a list of references in the handout so that members of the audience will be able to locate the speaker's sources of information.

The following information is usually provided in such documentation:

the name of the author, the title of the article or book, the name of the maga-zine or newspaper, the place of publication and the publisher of a book, the date of publication, and the page numbers. The required information varies according to the type of source (for example, a magazine or a book). The most common formats for references in the fields of English and speech are provided by the Modern Language Association (MLA) and the American Psychologi-cal Association (APA). For other fields (such as engineering or business), you should check with your colleagues or professors about the preferred format.

As you do research for your speech, be sure to make a note of all the information you will need for your references. Following is a list of references for a speech on English-only written according to the APA format (note that the list is presented in alphabetical order):

REFERENCES FOR "OPPOSING AN ENGLISH LANGUAGE AMENDMENT TO THE U.S. CONSTITUTION"

PAPER	Chen, E. M. (1986). *Proposition 63: An Unamerican Idea.* Paper presented at San Francisco State University.
BOOK (editor)	Daniels, H. A. (1990). The roots of protectionism. In H. A. Daniels (Ed.), *Not only English: Affirming America's multilingual heritage* (pp. 3–12). Urbana, IL: National Council of Teachers of English.
NEWSLETTER ARTICLE (unsigned)	Freedom of speech in Non-English languages upheld. (1989 May–August). *EPIC Events,* II (2–3). Newsletter of the English Plus Clearinghouse.
NEWSLETTER	Newsletter. (1990, January). I, (1). Newsletter of the National Coalition for Language Freedom.
NEWSPAPER ARTICLE (signed)	Stanwix, J. (1988, February 7). Our common language means equal opportunity for all. *Rochester Democrat and Chronicle,* p. A17.
NEWSPAPER ARTICLE (signed)	Trasvina, J. (1986, October 12). Bilingual Americans. *San Francisco Sunday Examiner and Chronicle,* p. A13.
NEWSPAPER EDITORIAL	Wright, G. (1986, October 12). *San Francisco Sunday Examiner and Chronicle,* p. A13.

Activity 4:   Organizing Reference Material

Organize the following reference material according to the APA format, and put the entries in the correct order.

> *San Francisco Sunday Examiner and Chronicle.* Nakao, A. Battle of words heats up over "English only." (September 21, 1986), pp. A1, A12.

> Vasquez, S. *Rochester Democrat and Chronicle,* p. A17. The diversity of our nation is the source of our strength. 1988, February 7.

> February 8, 1990. Judge nullifies law mandating use of English. Barringer, F. *The New York Times National,* pp. A1, B10.

> *English Today,* 1991, 31–35. English as a symbol of American culture. S. Nichols. 25.

Choosing Arguments to Support Your Position

After you have gathered and read through a variety of resource materials on your topic, you need to establish a clear purpose for your speech. In order to do so, it is a good idea to actually write out what you consider to be the purpose of your speech. For example, the speaker on English-only laws might write the following:

> **PURPOSE:**   To get the audience to agree that they should oppose an English-only amendment to the Constitution.

Once you are clear about the purpose of your speech, your next step is to select arguments to support your position. An important thing to consider in selecting your arguments is whether you have a sufficient amount of strong evidence to back them up. Your evidence should consist of facts and/or authoritative opinions, as indicated earlier in this unit.

There are several ways in which persuasive speeches may be organized: one is simply to give several arguments in support of your position; another is to first present your arguments and then counter some opposing arguments; a third is to follow each argument with an opposing argument and then counter that argument. Although there are other methods of organization besides

"Pro-choice" or "pro-life"? Whatever your position on the topic you choose for this speech, you need to gather information to support your arguments as well as to counter opposing arguments.

these three, we suggest using the second or third method of organization for this particular assignment.

In our example of a speech on an English-only amendment, the speaker selects the second method of organization. She chooses arguments that deal with human services and civil rights, bilingual education, and the lack of necessity for English-only laws. The speaker then thinks of important points that she will need to counter and comes up with the following: (1) people say that their parents/grandparents didn't have bilingual education and they did very well in school; and (2) if everyone spoke English, there would be less divisiveness in their community/city.

Organizing Your Arguments

The arguments that you have chosen will become the main points of your speech. As in your previous speeches, you will need to decide on the best order for presenting these points. For a persuasive speech, it is a good idea to start out with something that most members of your audience are likely to agree with in order to win them to your side. You can then move to a slightly more controversial point and present the most controversial points last. Applying this approach to English-only, the speaker is confident that her audience will support the idea of civil rights for everyone, but does not feel that the audience would be ready at the beginning of the speech for the argument that English-only laws are unnecessary. Therefore, she plans to use this argument as the last one and put bilingual education second. Finally, she will respond to the opposing arguments, so the organization of her main points might look like this:

ARGUMENTS

   I. English-only laws can deprive people of their civil rights

  II. They can eliminate bilingual education

 III. They are unnecessary

OPPOSING ARGUMENTS

 IV. People learned English in the past without bilingual education

  V. If everyone speaks English, greater unity will result

This brief outline shows one way of including opposing arguments in a persuasive speech. Another way, as previously mentioned, is to state each argument followed by your supporting evidence and then the opposing argument and countering response. Here is how the outline would look for the English-only speech:

   I. English-only laws can deprive people of their civil rights
     Supporting evidence
     Opposing argument—countering response

  II. English-only laws can eliminate bilingual education
     Supporting evidence
     Opposing argument—countering response

 III. English-only laws are unnecessary
     Supporting evidence
     Opposing argument—countering response

Activity 5:   Evaluating Your Classmates' Purpose and Arguments

For homework, write out the purpose of your speech and an outline of the arguments and opposing arguments you plan to present. Bring several copies to class. In small groups, take turns explaining your purpose and outline. Group members can use the following questions for discussion and evaluation:

1. Is the purpose of the speech clear and appropriate for the assignment?

2. Does the speaker have enough strong arguments?

3. Do the arguments relate equally to the purpose of the speech?

4. What is the rationale for the order of the arguments?

5. Has the speaker chosen important opposing arguments to counter?

Choosing Supporting Evidence

In selecting evidence and other kinds of information to support your arguments, you need to think about (1) how you can make your evidence convincing, and (2) how you can make it appeal to your audience.

Use sound reasoning   To convince your audience, it is extremely important that you use logical reasoning in support of your arguments. Three common types of reasoning are making generalizations, using analogy, and showing cause and effect.

When you make a **generalization,** you draw on several examples or pieces of information to draw a conclusion. For example, let's say 26,000 people are on waiting lists to get into English classes in New York, 17,000 in Philadelphia, and 12,000 in Detroit, and these three cities are in states with no English-only laws. Then we can say that immigrants are eager to learn English even though their states don't require them to do so.

Using an **analogy** to reason involves drawing a conclusion based on what happened in a similar situation. For example, if discrimination against non-English-speaking workers occurred in Colorado and Florida after English-only laws were passed in 1988, then we can assume it may occur in other states as well if an English-only amendment to the Constitution is passed.

You can use **cause-effect reasoning** to show that certain causes have certain effects. Your reasoning may focus on positive or negative effects. For example, you might show that passing English-only laws (cause) has resulted in reduced language services in hospitals and courts of law (negative effect). Or, you might show that students' receiving bilingual education (cause) has resulted in their developing strong self-esteem (positive effect).

Build your credibility   The quality of the evidence you present is extremely important in building the trust of your audience. Thus you should try to make sure that any claims you make are valid. Also, if you cite someone in support of one of your arguments, that person should be respected as an authority on the subject.

When using statistics as evidence, you must be sure that the conclusions you draw are based on **valid claims.** For instance, you might state that because only sixteen states have English language laws, most people in the United States would not support an amendment to the Constitution. However, many states may never have brought the matter to a vote, so this would not necessarily prove to be a valid conclusion. On the other hand, it might be reasonable to claim that New Mexico is more tolerant about language use than the sixteen states with English language laws because its constitution "guarantees that those who speak Spanish will be accommodated in the school system and in the courts." *

The speaker could cite **authority figures** to support an argument that English-only laws are unconstitutional using quotations from an article in *The New York Times National* of February 8, 1990. The article reports that federal judge Paul G. Rosenblatt declared Arizona's law mandating the use of English "a violation of federally protected free speech rights." She could continue by pointing out that the same article quoted the governor of Arizona, Rose Mofford, as saying "I am happy that the courts ruled it unconstitutional . . . the law was flawed from the beginning." †

Counter opposing arguments   As you prepared the outline of the main points of your speech, you included some arguments opposing your position. Remember that it is important to counter these arguments in order to show that they are either weak or false. For example, in the English-only speech, the speaker decides to raise the opposing argument that, in the past, students did well in school without the benefit of bilingual education. To counter this, the speaker uses information from the English-only article to make the point that, in the past, students were not as successful as people think. The article states, "In 1911, the U.S. Immigration Service found that 77 percent of Italian, 60

---

* Nichols, Steve, "English as a Symbol of American Culture," *English Today,* No. 25, January 1991, p. 31.

† Barringer, Felicity, "Judge Nullifies Law Mandating Use of English," *The New York Times National,* February 8, 1990, pp. A1, B10.

percent of Russian, and 51 percent of German immigrant children were one or more grade levels behind in school compared to 28 percent of American-born white children."

Make evidence clear and visual   No matter how strong your evidence is in favor of your position, if your audience doesn't understand it clearly, they won't be convinced. You want to find ways to make this information stand out so that it is easily understood and remembered. Two ways to do this are to make comparisons and to tell short anecdotes.

The author of the English-only article uses this first technique when he makes a comparison by talking about a "sink or swim" situation. He says, "The 'sink or swim' experience of past immigrants left more of them underwater than not." He is comparing non-English-speaking children in English-only classes to nonswimmers in deep water who have to either swim or drown. The speaker could use this comparison to help the audience understand and visualize the children's situation clearly: the audience could then see the children as swimmers, struggling to keep their heads above water, totally on their own with no life preservers for support.

The English-only article also includes a short anecdote about a Salvadoran mother who was able to save her child's life because of the coaching she received in Spanish from a 911 emergency operator. The speaker can retell this anecdote as a vivid illustration of the value of multilingual emergency services. The audience will be able to picture the desperate mother, her frantic call to 911, the careful directions of the Spanish-speaking dispatcher, and the actual resuscitation of the child as the siren wails in the distance. After this moving story, the speaker can then make her point by asking "What if this dispatcher had not been able to speak Spanish?"

Appealing to Your Audience

Once you have decided on some of the evidence you will use, your next task is to figure out how to present it in ways that will have the greatest appeal to your audience. From your survey, you are aware that some members of your audience agree with your position, some are neutral, and some oppose it. For those who agree with your position, you should try to present your arguments in such a way that you kindle their enthusiasm and motivate them to take action. For those who are neutral, you will need to provide adequate background information so that they can follow and be persuaded by your arguments. Regarding those who oppose your position, you should realize that it is difficult to change opposing attitudes and that you are not likely to do so in one short speech. A more realistic goal is to try to win opposing members' approval on perhaps one point and cause them to review their attitudes toward the others.

You can appeal to your audience and solicit their support in a variety of ways:

1. **Bring up things that you have in common with the audience.** For instance, in a speech opposing English-only laws, a speaker could point out in his introduction that English is a second language for everyone in the audience, and that all members of the audience undoubtedly value their own languages and enjoy speaking and writing them.

2. **Appeal to values that most people share.** For example, most people believe in human rights, so in defense of her argument about human rights, the speaker might quote and paraphrase from the article as follows:

   > As the ACLU points out, quote, such laws are contrary to the spirit of tolerance and diversity embodied in our Constitution, end of quote. The ACLU feels that an English language amendment to the Constitution would change the basic nature of the Constitution. It would no longer protect individual freedoms but would restrict them.

3. **Point out how opposing your position may have undesirable results.** You can arouse a certain amount of fear of what may happen if audience members do *not* support your position. In this case, the speaker might mention the possibility of 911 services, medical services, or court translation services not being offered in any language besides English if the constitutional amendment is passed. She might go on to say that while the lack of such services may not affect audience members themselves, it is likely that this might cause serious difficulties for older members of their families.

4. **Show how supporting your position will be beneficial.** For example, here are several points the speaker could make. If people can continue to use their own language freely, they can still advertise and celebrate ethnic activities using their own language as well as English. Family members who do not have a strong command of English can benefit from multilingual human services and will still be able to find employment if English is not made a compulsory language in the workplace. Furthermore, bilingual education will still be available to immigrant children when they first arrive in the United States.

5. **Appeal to your audience's emotions as well as their intellect.** According to Charles Larson, author of a book on persuasion, there are two kinds of evidence. One kind has an **emotional appeal** directed at the audience's feelings, imagination, and empathy; the other has a **rational appeal** directed at the audience's intellect.* Because we probably all like to think of ourselves as rational people, we might conclude that it is preferable to use only rational kinds of evidence in our speeches. However, some research has shown that intellectual knowledge alone rarely moves people to action. The kind of evidence you use may also depend on the issue you are arguing. On some issues, people may be more easily convinced by evidence with an emotional appeal, whereas on other issues, people may be more easily convinced by evidence with an intellectual appeal. Thus you'll probably be better off using both kinds of evidence because listeners may vary considerably in the type of evidence that will motivate them.

Let's look at how emotional and rational appeals have been used to defend and oppose English-only laws. In his article "English as a Symbol of American Culture," Steve Nichols observes that "groups in favor of making English the official language of the United States . . . have relied on emotional appeals to gain support." Following is one of his examples taken from a letter from the American Ethnic Coalition:

> **EXAMPLE OF AN EMOTIONAL APPEAL:**   Now, America is increasingly populated by illegal immigrants and other factions who look upon America's English language as a secondary language and who cling to their ethnicity so strongly as to do both themselves and America a great disservice.

Nichols continues, "Groups which have opposed making English the official language have used more rational claims in their defense against official English. Most of the claims of these organizations are aimed at countering the claims of the pro-official English groups." This example of a rational approach comes from the Statement of Purpose of EPIC (English Plus Information Clearinghouse):

> **EXAMPLE OF A RATIONAL APPEAL:**   "English Plus" rejects the ideology and divisive character of the so-called "English Only"

---

*Larson, Charles U., *Persuasion: Reception and Responsibility* (Belmont, CA: Wadsworth, 1983), pp. 106–10.

movement. "English Plus" holds that national unity and our constitutional values require that language assistance be made available in order to ensure equal access to essential services, education, the electoral process, and other rights and opportunities guaranteed to all members of society.

For Discussion

1. What are three common types of reasoning? Give an example of each type.

2. In what ways can a speaker build credibility with an audience?

3. How can a speaker make certain pieces of evidence stand out?

4. What can a speaker do to interest audience members who are neutral about his or her position on the speech topic?

5. What are some ways that a speaker can present evidence to appeal to an audience? Give examples.

6. What is the difference between an emotional appeal and a rational appeal? Give an example of each.

Outlining the Body of Your Speech

Once you have selected the most effective evidence and figured out how to make it appeal to your audience, your next step is to prepare a complete outline of the body of your speech. A sample outline of the speech opposing an English language amendment to the U.S. Constitution follows:

ARGUMENTS

    I. English-only laws can deprive people of their civil rights
        A. Opportunity to get emergency/medical/community help
            1. 911 services
            2. Translation services for doctors and hospitals
            3. Driver's license handbooks
            4. Notices from children's schools

    B. Opportunity to get a fair trial

        1. Defendant unable to understand charges or answer them

        2. Witnesses unable to provide evidence

        3. Victims unable to explain what has happened to them

    C. Ability to understand voting materials

        1. Issues often complicated

        2. Language difficult—even for native speakers

II. English-only laws can eliminate bilingual education

    A. Effects of such laws on legislators' views of learning in a language besides English

    B. Research on bilingual education

        1. Previous results questionable

        2. Recent research—bilingual ed. beneficial—example

III. English-only laws are unnecessary

    A. Importance of English already well established

        1. Language of education

        2. Language of commerce

        3. Language of government

    B. Immigrants anxious to learn English without English-only laws

        1. Thousands on waiting lists for classes in New York and Los Angeles (NCLF)

        2. Over 95 percent first-generation Mexican-Americans English proficient

    C. Only effect of laws—negative for poor and elderly

OPPOSING ARGUMENTS

IV. Previous immigrants did not have bilingual education

    A. Some successful, but others not—example

    B. Job market in the past vs. today

        1. Past—more limited education—enough for job market

        2. Today—more technical skills needed

V. English-only laws promote unity and harmony

    A. Resentment from enforcement of such laws in the workplace

        1. Florida supermarket checker (Daniels)

        2. Denver restaurant worker (Daniels)

B. Narrow perspective created
   1. Alternative approaches to problem-solving lost
   2. Cultural traditions diminish—1980 Dade County, Florida, barred funds promoting non-American culture
C. Broader perspective valuable
   1. Global village—international affairs and business
   2. Sharing of language and cultural traditions of benefit to everyone

---

Activity 6:   Evaluating Evidence

Using the outline for the body of the English-only speech, answer the following questions for homework. In small groups, review your answers and be prepared to discuss them with the class.

1. What evidence could be presented as a generalization? As cause-effect reasoning?

2. What evidence could build the speaker's credibility?

3. What evidence does the speaker use to counter the opposing arguments? Does the evidence provide a convincing response?

4. Where could the speaker use evidence to appeal to values most people share? To point out negative consequences of opposing views? To show how the audience can benefit from supporting her position?

5. What evidence could be used to appeal to the audience's emotions? To their intellects?

Activity 7:   Evaluating Your Classmates' Evidence

For homework, prepare an outline of the body of your speech. Bring several copies to class, and in small groups do the following:

1. Consider whether the supporting evidence in each outline is sufficient and appropriate. If not, give suggestions about additional material the speaker should look for.

2. Use the questions listed in Activity 6 to help the speaker plan his or her speech.

Making Transitions

All the information presented in Unit 3 on transitions is relevant to your persuasive speech. However, you are likely to use more transitions that show contrast in a persuasive speech than in a demonstration speech. Countering opposing arguments frequently calls for transitions that indicate contrast.

Following are lists of four different kinds of transitions that you can use to show contrast and sentences with an example of each type.

although	but	instead of	however
even though	yet	in spite of	in contrast
even if		despite	on the contrary
while			to the contrary
whereas			conversely
			on the other hand

EXAMPLES:

<u>Although</u> some people claim that immigrants don't want to learn English, documentation shows that 26,000 adults are on waiting lists for English classes in New York and 40,000 in Los Angeles.

Some city governments have recently claimed that they do not have sufficient funds to provide translators in city hospitals; <u>yet</u> patients' health, and sometimes even their lives, may be threatened.

<u>Despite</u> the need for speakers of other languages in business and international affairs, English-only supporters usually oppose bilingual education.

Some business owners say that if all employees are required to speak English, job performance will improve; <u>instead</u>, the requirement causes low morale so production drops.

Activity 8:   Practicing Transitions

Using the outline for the body of "In Opposition to an English Language Amendment to the U.S. Constitution," do the following:

1. Make up a rhetorical question to introduce the argument stated in part I.

2. Summarize the arguments stated in parts I and II as you introduce part III.

3. Make a transition from the argument section of the speech (parts I, II, and III) as you introduce the first opposing argument (part IV).

4. For argument B in part IV, use a transition that expresses contrast to move from point 1 to point 2.

Preparing Your Conclusion

In ending your speech, you first need to summarize the arguments you have presented in favor of your position. Next comes the part of the conclusion that is especially important in a persuasive speech—the appeal to your audience. If you want your audience to support you in taking action, the conclusion offers a final opportunity to motivate them, so you should try to make your appeal as effective and as hard to refuse as possible. You should also be very specific about what you want your audience to do. You may stress the benefits of following the action you recommend or, alternatively, the harmful effects that may result if action is not taken to support your proposition. Finally, try to make your closing words both powerful and memorable.

Activity 9:   Evaluating Conclusions

Determine which of the following would be the most effective conclusion for the speech "In Opposition to an English Language Amendment to the U.S. Constitution." Consider whether each conclusion (1) provides an adequate summary of the speaker's arguments, (2) enlists the audience's support and/or motivates them to action, and (3) has a powerful and memorable ending.

a. So, when you consider everything I've told you, you should realize that it is really important to let your legislators know that making this amendment to the Constitution is not a good idea. You should, therefore, write and tell them about your opposition to it.

b. In conclusion, I'm quite sure that none of you would want to jeopardize the civil rights of others. I know that you want the best possible education for all children in the U.S. And I'm convinced that you understand that real unity comes from preserving and respecting all the cultures represented here. Therefore, I'm now going to hand out a sheet with the names and addresses of your legislators so that you can write to them today and let them know how harmful an English language amendment would be. Let us together oppose this misguided attempt to shatter our unity with our own unified stand for freedom of language use for all.

c. To sum up, I have pointed out some of the possible harmful effects of an English language amendment to the Constitution. I certainly hope that you agree with me after hearing my speech.

Activity 10:   *Evaluating Your Classmates' Conclusions*

For homework, prepare the conclusion to your speech in an outline or on note cards. Then in small groups, listen to and evaluate each conclusion. Listen more than once if necessary and give suggestions for improvement as needed. Here are some suggested questions for evaluation:

1. Does the conclusion summarize the speaker's arguments? What are the arguments?

2. How does the speaker appeal to the audience for their support?

3. What makes the speaker's ending strong?

Preparing Your Introduction

It is always important to grab your audience's attention at the beginning of a speech, but in a persuasive speech, you also need to try to elicit their support right from the beginning. You can usually find at least one aspect of your topic that most people will agree with, so you can begin by emphasizing it. For instance, you might begin a speech opposing English-only laws by describing how a 911 dispatcher helped a mother save her child's life because she was able to provide instructions to the mother in Spanish. Your attention-getter should, of course, lead smoothly into the introduction of your topic. In a persuasive speech, your introduction should include sufficient background material to enable your audience to follow your arguments. Therefore, it will be longer than the introduction to your informative speech. You will also need to establish your credibility as a speaker from the beginning of your speech (see page 174) and make your position on the speech topic clear to your listeners.

Activity 11:   *Evaluating Introductions*

Determine which of the following would be the most effective introduction for the speech "In Opposition to an English Language Amendment to the U.S. Constitution." You may use the following questions to help you evaluate:

1. How does the opening grab the audience's attention and win their support?

2. What background material does the speaker include in the introduction?

3. How does the speaker establish credibility?

4. What is the speaker's position on the topic?

a. Several English language amendments to the U.S. Constitution have already been proposed, but so far they have remained in committee and have never been brought to a vote. However, laws concerning the use of English have now been passed in sixteen states. The first of those laws was passed in Nebraska in 1923, the second in Illinois in 1969, and all the others in the 1980s. The people who voted for these laws, and perhaps some of you, might think that an English language amendment would benefit the United States; but, today, I hope to convince you that such an amendment would do more harm than good.

b. I am sure you would all agree that we should protect every citizen's civil rights, that we should give every child the best possible education, and that we should respect the cultures of the different ethnic groups that make up the United States. Since we are all in agreement, you may wonder why I have chosen to begin my speech in this way. Well, today I'm going to explain to you how these basic elements of our democratic society may soon be jeopardized.

c. A story in the *Washington Times* reported in 1987 that a 911 emergency dispatcher was able to help a Salvadoran woman save the life of her baby son by coaching the woman in Spanish over the telephone on what to do until the paramedics arrived. It certainly is not difficult for you to imagine what would probably have happened if the 911 dispatcher had not been able to speak Spanish. Well, it may surprise you to learn that some people are proposing an amendment to the U.S. Constitution that could mean the end of such foreign language services. In fact, a number of states in the United States have already passed English-only laws that have affected services provided in languages other than English. A total of fourteen states, including California and Florida, which have large immigrant populations, passed such laws during the 1980s. Through my research, I have learned about the various effects that these laws can have. Therefore, today I plan to explain to you how such an amendment could not only affect vital human services but also have many other harmful effects on our society, and to enlist your support in preventing its becoming law.

Activity 12:   Evaluating Your Classmates' Introductions

For homework, prepare an introduction to your speech in an outline or on note cards. Then, in small groups, listen to and evaluate each introduction. Listen more than once if necessary and give suggestions for improvement as needed. You may use the questions in Activity 11 for evaluation.

PRESENTING YOUR SPEECH

You will obviously be more successful in persuading your audience to accept your position if you are able to deliver your arguments convincingly (see page 177). To make your delivery expressive, you might try these techniques: (1) change the volume and tone of your voice at appropriate times, (2) pause for a little longer than usual in order to focus the audience's attention, and (3) use effective gestures to help illustrate and emphasize important points.

Remember that good visual aids can also help to make your speech convincing. For example, graphs and charts can support rational appeals to your audience; pictures and slides can support emotional appeals. Think carefully about the kinds of visual aids that will have the greatest impact on your audience for your particular arguments, and choose those that strengthen your appeals.

Effective gestures can help illustrate and emphasize important points and thus make your arguments convincing.

LISTENING AND EVALUATING

Before members of the class start to give their speeches, you will need to review the evaluation criteria on the form that follows Activity 13. As you evaluate a speech, consider whether the speaker has provided enough background material for you to follow the speech. Then listen for the speaker's point of view about the topic. Were the speaker's arguments clear and supported by sufficiently strong evidence? Did the speaker counter opposing arguments? Were the references to source materials clear? Did the speaker present his or her arguments in a way that was likely to convince the audience?

Activity 13:   Reporting on a Persuasive Speech

Choose a persuasive speech that you considered to be especially convincing and report on it. You may want to do the following in your report:

1. Provide an introduction in which you state whose speech you are evaluating, the topic of the speech, and the speaker's point of view about the topic.

2. List background information about the topic.

3. Give reasons why the speaker's arguments were convincing.

4. Provide a conclusion in which you state whether the speaker reinforced your own opinion about the topic or brought about a change in your point of view.

Unit 6   Persuasive Speech

Speaker _____

Evaluator _____

Topic _____

RATING SYSTEM: + = excellent
√ — average
— = weak

Content/Organization/Preparation

_____ Opening attracted listeners' attention.

_____ Background information was sufficient.

_____ Speaker's point of view was clear.

_____ Arguments were clear. List below.

     1. _____

       _____

     2. _____

       _____

     3. _____

       _____

_____ Evidence was convincing.

_____ Opposing arguments were countered well.

_____ Appropriate transitions were used.

_____ References to source materials were adequate.

_____ Speech had a suitable conclusion.

_____ Visual aids were effective.

_____ Content fit time limit.

Presentation/Delivery

_____ Eye contact

_____ Vitality

_____ Gestures

_____ Rapport with audience

_____ Spoke convincingly

_____ Use of note cards or outline

VOICE CONTROL:

_____ Volume

_____ Rate

_____ Fluency

_____ Comprehensibility

Comments and suggestions for improvement:

PARTICIPATING IN PANEL DISCUSSIONS

A panel discussion is a format for persuasive speaking in which two sides of an issue are argued. For example, if an English language amendment to the Constitution were the discussion topic, then some members of the panel would argue in favor of the amendment and others against it.

How will this work? Several members of the class will form a group (let's call them team A) to take a stand on a particular issue and argue in favor of that position. Several other members of the class will form another group, team B, which will take the opposite stand on the issue and will argue in favor of their position. These teams will present their arguments in the form of a panel discussion. There will be more than one panel discussion so that all members of the class will have a chance to participate. Prior to the presentations, each team will meet to discuss their ideas, to come up with evidence to support their opinions, and to plan their presentation. During the presentations, the entire class will serve as the audience and will have a chance to ask questions when both sides have finished their presentations and questioned each other.

In this activity you will have a chance to use all your diplomacy and politeness to argue for your position and against another position. More specifically, participating in a panel discussion will give you a chance to practice many of the skills you have been working on in this course. First of all, when preparing your presentation for the panel, you will have to use your communication skills to discuss the issue in question and to reach a consensus on the arguments for your position and on ways to support those arguments. You will need to anticipate the ideas that the opposite team will think of and have responses ready to meet those points. You will have to use your organization skills to plan your presentation.

When making your presentation, you must draw on what you have learned about effective delivery, use of visual aids, and active listening. In addition, you will have to "think on your feet" when answering the questions from the opposing team and from the audience. Although this sounds like a lot to worry about, most students find this activity challenging and exciting.

Suggested Procedure

A panel discussion can have a variety of formats. We suggest the following procedure for your panels:

For a panel discussion, a moderator introduces the two teams, who then present and defend opposing positions on an issue.

1. Team A opens the discussion. The members will each speak for an equal amount of time, dividing up the content (introduction, main and supporting points, and conclusion) as they see appropriate. (Suggested time: six to nine minutes.)

2. Team B presents its side of the issue in an identical manner. (Suggested time: six to nine minutes.) (*Note:* During these initial presentations, panel members should be taking notes on the other team's ideas so that they can formulate relevant questions.)

3. Team A questions team B about its main points. (Suggested time: two to four minutes.)

4. Team B questions team A about its main points. (Suggested time: two to four minutes.)

5. One member of team A briefly summarizes the team's main points. (Suggested time: one minute.)

6. One member of team B briefly summarizes the team's main points. (Suggested time: one minute.)

7. Members of the audience may question either team A or team B (as time permits).

A panel discussion always has a moderator to control the discussion. The duties of the moderator are as follows:

- At the beginning, to announce the topic and introduce the panel members.

- To introduce the various steps of the proceedings. (For example, the moderator can say, "Now that we have heard team A's position, we will hear team B's view.")

- Throughout the discussion, to keep track of the main points and questions so that they can be restated if someone doesn't understand. (The moderator may ask a panel member for restatement whenever necessary.)

- To watch the time closely and make sure that everyone stays within the time limits. The moderator might say one of the following:

  Please limit your answer to thirty seconds.

  You have one minute to summarize.

  I'm sorry to interrupt you but we are out of time.

- To make sure that everyone has a chance to speak. This includes calling on those who haven't yet asked or answered questions and asking panel members to stop talking so that others can speak.

- To *avoid* giving his or her own opinion or showing bias for either side.

Responding to Other Views

You will have a chance to respond to the other team's ideas in two ways during the question/answer session: you will have to answer their questions about your position and evidence, and you will be able to ask them questions about their position and evidence.

We said earlier that when planning your presentation, you should consider the audience's attitudes and think about ways in which they would disagree with your position. In your presentation, your team should try to take these objections into account and counter them. However, if you do not have time to cover all these objections in your presentation, then you can be certain that the other team will raise them during the question/answer period. So, as part of your planning for the presentation, a good strategy would be to *predict* the questions that the other team will ask you and then plan out what your answers will be.

In Unit 4, in the section "Keeping Your Discussion on Track," we talked about ways you can relate your contribution to that of others and ways to show agreement and disagreement. (Review that unit now if you have forgotten those strategies.) The following are some suggestions for asking questions of the other team:

1. **While the other team is speaking, take notes of the ideas and evidence they use that you wish to question them about.** Be sure to write down the name of the individual making the point so that you can direct your question to that person. For example, you might say,

   > I have a question for Ali. Ali, in your presentation, you said that. . . . My question is . . .

2. **Pay careful attention to the evidence that the other team uses and question them if it does not seem sufficient to you.** If the other team has made a general statement with no supporting evidence, then question them about their lack of evidence. For example, you could say,

   > Mariko, you said. . . . I would like to know what evidence you might have to support this statement.

   Note the polite forms used. The speaker does *not* say,

   > No, you're wrong! Tell me your evidence!

3. **In general, use the question/answer period to obtain additional information.** For example, you might want to request more evidence, clarification of evidence, or clarification of how the evidence logically supports the argument. Some expressions you might use include the following:

I wonder if you could clarify . . .

Could you please explain what the relationship is between . . . and . . .

Would you please expand on your reasons for believing that . . .

I'm sure we could understand your position better if you could just give us some concrete evidence to show that . . .

LISTENING AND EVALUATING

Listen carefully and take notes on the arguments and evidence that each team presents. Consider whether they seem convincing. Also pay close attention to the questions and responses to determine whether or not they are to the point and support the team's position. The two evaluation forms at the end of the unit—one for individuals and one for groups—should be used to help you as you evaluate.

Activity 14:   Reporting on a Panel Discussion

For this assignment, choose one of the panel discussions presented in class, and prepare a report as follows:

1. State the issue discussed.

2. State the position taken by team A, summarize the main points they made, and describe the evidence they used to support their points. In stating the position, you can use expressions such as the following:

   Team A <u>took the position that</u> an English language amendment to the U.S. Constitution would . . .

   Team A <u>argued that</u> . . .

   <u>Team A's position was that</u> . . .

   Team A <u>supported the belief that</u> . . . (*not* "Team A believed that . . .")

3. State the position taken by team B, summarize the main points they made, and describe the evidence they used to support their points.

4. Summarize any interesting points that came up during the question/answer period.

5. Tell which team's presentation you found more convincing, and why. (*Note:* The fact that you agreed with their position is not a sufficient reason to find their presentation convincing!) Consider such points as the team's organization of ideas, their evidence, their ability to respond to questions, and their speech delivery.

Unit 6   Panel Discussion: Individual Evaluation

Speaker _____

Evaluator _____

Topic _____

RATING SYSTEM: + = excellent
$\sqrt{}$ = average
− = weak

Content/Organization/Preparation

_____ Arguments were clear.

_____ Arguments had strong supporting evidence.

_____ Evidence was convincing.

_____ Transitions from previous speaker and to next speaker were smooth.

_____ Speaker asked relevant questions.

_____ Speaker responded to questions well.

Presentation/Delivery

_____ Eye contact

_____ Vitality

_____ Rapport with audience

_____ Spoke convincingly

_____ Use of note cards or outline

VOICE CONTROL:

_____ Volume

_____ Rate

_____ Fluency

_____ Comprehensibility

Comments and suggestions for improvement:

Unit 6   Panel Discussion: Group Evaluation

Group _____

Evaluator _____

Topic _____

RATING SYSTEM: + = excellent
                 √ = average
                 − = weak

_____ Introduction was effective.

_____ Arguments were clear.

_____ Arguments had strong supporting evidence.

_____ Evidence was convincing.

_____ Transitions between speakers were good.

_____ Conclusion was effective.

_____ Visual aids were effective.

_____ Presentation was well balanced among speakers.

_____ Content fit the time limit.

_____ Panel asked relevant questions.

_____ Panel responded to questions well.

_____ Participation was approximately equal in the question/answer period.

List the team's arguments:

Comments:

Appendix

Pronunciation

SPEAKING CLEARLY: RATE, PAUSES, PHRASE GROUPING, AND EMPHASIS

To communicate effectively, not only must the *content* of your message be clear, but the *form* of the message must be clear as well. By working on your pronunciation skills, you can improve the form of your communication. This appendix provides information and exercises in several areas of English pronunciation that are often a problem for non-native speakers of English.

Although the individual sounds of English are important, other features of oral production are often more important for making yourself understood. In this section, we will consider three features of pronunciation that can make a crucial difference in getting your message across. These three features—rate of speech, pauses and phrase grouping of words, and emphasis—are inter-related, but we will consider each of them individually.

Rate of Speech

Many of us who lack confidence about speaking in front of a group make the mistake of speaking too quickly. Often, non-native speakers of English worry that they lack fluency in English, and so they try to speak quickly to make up for it. But that doesn't solve the problem; it just makes it more difficult for listeners to understand them. Also, many people tend to speak more rapidly than normal when in front of a group, just because they are nervous.

So most of you should think, first of all, about slowing down! Start listening to your professors when they give assignments or lecture to the class; start listening to your fellow workers when they make presentations, dictate letters, or explain a problem to the boss. In such situations, individuals are using the spoken language for primarily a *transactional* function—that is, for

223

the communication of a message. This is quite different from the way individuals use the spoken language in conversations that serve to maintain social relations. This is often referred to as the *interactional* function of language.

In "transactional talk," the speaker tends to speak more slowly than in "interactional talk." This doesn't mean just slowing down and saying every word more slowly; it means saying key words more slowly and emphasizing them, and it means pausing more often. These points are discussed further in the following sections.

Pauses and Phrase Grouping

Spoken English has rules regarding the grouping of words into phrases. Slight pauses come between these phrase groups. Consider the sentences in the following example:

> To communicate effectively, / you have to be careful / just how you group / the words you use. / / You should group words together / that are related / in grammar and meaning. / /

A slash (/) sets off phrase groups and indicates where slight pauses occur. A double slash (/ /) indicates slightly longer pauses at the ends of sentences. Listen while your teacher reads the example sentences. Now, as your teacher reads them a second time, at a slightly faster pace, notice that the pause between "group" and "the" disappears, as does the pause between "related" and "in." This is because when you speak faster, you include more words in a phrase group. Now listen while your teacher reads the sentences above with inappropriate pauses and phrase groups and see how difficult they are to understand.

Activity 1:   Marking Phrase Groupings

In the following sentences, place a slash (/) between the phrase groups.

a. Effective communication, which is important in every field, is not as easy as many people think.

b. Today many large corporations in the United States have special seminars to train their employees to be better communicators.

c. It's too bad such employees can't take this oral communication course: they could save their companies lots of money!

Can you discover the rules determining which words to group together? Here are some rules and examples:

- Nouns + their modifiers: "in every field" and "many large corporations."

- Subject + verb combinations (and sometimes objects): "it's too bad" and "they could save their companies" and "you should group words together."

- Verb complement phrases: "to be better communicators."

- Noun modifiers following the noun: "seminars / to train their employees." *But note:* short restrictive relative clauses group *with* their nouns: "the words you use." Nonrestrictive relative clauses are always *separated* from the nouns they modify: "My brother, / who is an engineer, / . . ."

- Introductory words, phrases, and clauses: "to communicate effectively" and "today."

Emphasis

As noted previously, in transactional speech, the speaker will emphasize important words. But emphasizing important words is part of conversational, interactional speech, too. The question is, then, how do you know which words are the "important" words to emphasize?

Let's look at the sentences from the example on page 224 again. Which words do you think should be emphasized? Underline them.

To communicate effectively, you have to be careful just how you group the words you use. You should group words together that are related in grammar and meaning.

Here are some pointers about emphasis in English:

- **We give the most emphasis to the last important word or words in the sentence.** And by important, we generally mean a content word (a noun, verb, adjective, or adverb). In the example sentence, these important words are "use," "grammar," and "meaning." These words carry the important pitch change in the sentences. (Your voice starts at a higher pitch on "use" than on "you" and then drops as you pronounce the vowel *u* in "use." In the second sentence, your voice goes up to a higher pitch on *gra* and *mea* and then drops low on *mar* and *ning*. Which are the most important words in the sentences in Activity 1?

- **More than one word is emphasized in a sentence.** In fact, there will be at least one emphasized word in every phrase group, and there may be more than one. Again, the rule is to emphasize content words (nouns, verbs, adjectives, and adverbs) and not structure words (prepositions, pronouns, auxiliaries, conjunctions, articles).

    So, in the example sentences, most people would emphasize these words: "effectively," "careful," "group," "use," "together," "related," "grammar," "meaning." What kind of content word is each? (For example, "effectively" is an adverb.)

    As we said earlier, sometimes it is possible to emphasize more than one word in a phrase group. For example, in the first sentence, it would be possible to emphasize "communicate" and "effectively." In the second sentence both "grammar" and "meaning" receive emphasis.

    To give emphasis to a word, you must give emphasis to the stressed syllable in the word (if the word has more than one syllable) by saying this syllable more loudly, for a slightly longer time, and at a higher pitch from the surrounding syllables.

    Say these words: e<u>ffec</u>tively   <u>care</u>ful   to<u>geth</u>er   re<u>lat</u>ed

    Select the other words that should receive emphasis in the sentences in Activity 1 and practice pronouncing them.

- **It is possible to shift the emphasis in a sentence from what would normally be the important content word to any other word in the sentence:** We do this when we want to show contrast.

    It's too bad such employees can't take this oral communication course. They could save their companies lots of money! But they <u>don't</u> take this course, so communication skills end up costing <u>every</u>body a lot of money, not just the companies.

In the last sentence, two structure words are emphasized ("don't" and "everybody"). In both cases, the emphasis shows a contrast.

ASSIGNMENT: READING A PREPARED STATEMENT

This assignment will give you practice in reading a prepared statement in front of the class, allowing you to work on rate, pausing, and emphasis. Choose one of the following idioms and present it to the class. To prepare for this presentation, do the following:

1. Copy the text onto note cards, writing in sufficiently large print so that you can see it easily. We suggest you put only one sentence on each note card. Leave space so that you can mark the phrase groups by putting a slash (/) between the groups and a double slash (/ /) at the end of each sentence for a longer pause. (These pause marks are indicated in the first statement.)

2. Mark the emphasis by underlining the stressed syllable. (This emphasis is indicated for you in the first statement.)

3. Practice reading your statement at home. If you have a tape recorder, you might tape yourself and then listen critically to your reading. As you practice, focus on these things: (1) rate of speech, (2) correct word grouping and pauses, and (3) emphasis on appropriate words.

4. When you present your idiom to the class, write the idiom on the blackboard. Begin by looking at your audience and giving a short introduction, such as "Today, I'm going to tell you about the idiom . . ." Look at your audience as much as possible; don't bury your face in your note cards. Speak loudly enough so that everyone can hear you.

These ten idioms are taken from a list that appears in the appendix of *Cultural Literacy: What Every American Needs to Know,* by E. D. Hirsch, Jr.* The explanations and examples have been added by the authors of this book.

1. *back to the drawing board:*

A <u>draw</u>ing board is literally a <u>sur</u>face, / much like a <u>desk</u>, / where you <u>draw</u> something, / such as an illus<u>tra</u>tion or a <u>dia</u>gram. / / <u>So</u>, / by ex<u>ten</u>sion, / a <u>draw</u>ing board is a <u>place</u> where you <u>plan</u> / and work out <u>de</u>tails of something: / / it <u>could</u> be where you <u>write</u> a <u>pa</u>per, / where you <u>do</u> your ac<u>count</u>ing homework, / and <u>so</u> forth. / / So the ex<u>pres</u>sion / "<u>back</u> to the <u>draw</u>ing board" / means to re<u>turn</u> to the drawing board, / literally / to <u>start</u> <u>over</u>. / / It means be<u>gin</u>ning a<u>gain</u> on a project / because it didn't suc<u>ceed</u> / or wasn't quite <u>right</u>. / / <u>Here's</u> an e<u>xam</u>ple. / / Let's say <u>you</u> and several

---

* E. D. Hirsch, Jr., is a professor of English at the University of Virginia. In his controversial book, he argues that it is necessary for all students to have a core of background knowledge in order to make sense of what they read. In addition to numerous literary, scientific, and historical terms and people, dates, and quotations that students must know, Hirsch also lists a number of idioms. For further information, see *The Dictionary of Cultural Literacy* by E. D. Hirsch, Jr., Joseph Kett, and James Trefil (Boston: Houghton Mifflin, 1989).

classmates are working on a group <u>project</u> / for your <u>man</u>agement class. / / You <u>work</u> out an <u>outline</u> / and take it to your pro<u>fess</u>or. / / He looks it <u>over</u> / and <u>tells</u> you / you have done it <u>wrong</u>. / / You might <u>say</u> to your <u>class</u>mates, / "<u>Well</u>, / <u>back</u> to the <u>draw</u>ing board."

2. *to bite the bullet:* This expression means to face a difficult or painful situation bravely. It has a historical origin. In the days before anesthetics, it was a practice for soldiers to bite on a bullet when they were wounded and had to have surgery. This kept them from screaming out in pain. Nowadays you might hear the expression in a context like the following one. A friend tells you that he has been putting off telling his boss that he is going to quit because he has been offered a better job. He says that he hates to quit at this time because he knows that his boss is counting on him to work during the holidays but that he can't afford to pass up the job he has been offered. You say, "Well, you'll just have to bite the bullet and tell him."

3. *the bottom line:* This expression should be an easy one for those of you in accounting. The bottom line is literally the lowest line in a financial statement; it shows the net income or loss. Thus, the expression has come to mean the end result or the final effect of something. Here is a situation in which you might hear this expression. You have a part-time job and have recently been late for work on several occasions because you have had so much schoolwork to do. Your supervisor comes up to you and says, "The bottom line is this: If you don't start getting to work on time, you'll be fired." Here's another situation. It is the first day of the semester, and your professor is explaining the course requirements. He concludes by saying, "You must pass both the midterm and the final, or you will not pass the course. That's the bottom line."

4. *to cool one's heels:* This expression means to be kept waiting for someone or something. Here's an example. You have made an appointment to speak to your professor during her office hours right after class. So, after class, you rush to her office to keep your appointment. (Figuratively, your heels are hot from your fast walk to get there on time.) But when you arrive, she tells you you'll have to wait while she makes some telephone calls. The calls take fifteen minutes or so. Later you tell a friend that you had to cool your heels for fifteen minutes outside your professor's office door while she made some telephone calls.

5. *to play it by ear:* To play a musical instrument like a piano or a guitar by ear means to play the music by remembering how it sounds rather

than by reading the notes written on a sheet of music. So, by extension, this idiom means to do something without a planned course of action, to do something spontaneously by seeing how things are at the moment. Here's an example. Let's say you and a friend are going on a short trip for the weekend to a nearby tourist attraction. You ask your friend, "Should we make reservations at that Hungarian restaurant for Saturday night?" Your friend might say, "No, let's just play it by ear. Who knows? We might feel like eating Chinese food."

6. *to know the ropes:* This expression probably comes from sailing. In this case, "knowing the ropes" means knowing which ropes to tighten or loosen to get the sails up and down to control the ship's movement. So this expression means to know the way to do things, to be able to operate within a system, to understand how things work. Our school is a good example of a system in which it is important to know the ropes. For example, you may be confused about how to get a place in a class if you are on the waiting list, but another student who "knows the ropes" can give you good tips on what to do.

7. *to draw the line:* This expression means to set a limit, as on what behavior you are willing to accept or action you are willing to take. For example, suppose you have a car but your brother doesn't, so he always wants you to take him places. You might say, "Listen. I'll take you to school and I'll bring you back home, but that's where I draw the line. I will not take you to your girlfriend's house." Or your English tutor might say, "I see my job as helping you understand your assignments, but I won't do your assignments for you. That's where I draw the line."

8. *to read between the lines:* Here, the lines refer to lines of words that are being read. When you read between the lines, you pay attention to what is implied though not explicitly stated in the writing. By extension, this can refer to what is said as well as what is written. Here is an example. You have just read an article in the campus newspaper and tell your friend, "I know this article says that there will be no tuition increase in the coming year, but if you read between the lines, it is clear that they will find another way to make students pay more money."

9. *to spread oneself too thin:* Think of spreading butter on a piece of bread. If you spread it very thin, then you don't taste much butter, do you? Thus, if you spread yourself too thin, it means you are doing so many things at one time that you really can't do any of them very well. This is a common problem for students. If you are trying to work thirty

hours a week, take five courses, do your exercise routine for an hour a day, and keep up your relationship with your girlfriend or boyfriend, you may be spreading yourself too thin.

10. *the tip of the iceberg:* The major part of an iceberg is hidden beneath the water and only a small part of it, the tip, is visible above the surface of the water. So the tip of the iceberg refers to something that is only a hint or suggestion of a much larger or more complex issue or problem. For example, suppose you and your friend have just watched a TV news report about a series of bank failures. Your friend, who is a business major, might say, "And that's just the tip of the iceberg. Things are going to get a lot worse before they get better."

FINAL *S*

It is important that you pronounce the *s* at the end of present tense verbs in the third-person singular (think*s*). You also need to pronounce the final *s* in plural nouns (some opinion*s*) and possessives (the author'*s* book). If you don't pronounce the final *s* sound of words, you will be making not just pronunciation errors but grammatical errors as well. Look at this sentence:

> Dr. E. D. Hirsch argue*s* that it is necessary for all student*s* to know certain cultural concept*s* in order to make sense of what they read. In his book, he list*s* a number of idiom*s* which you might like to study.

If you were to say this sentence without pronouncing the underlined *s* sounds, you would be making a number of grammatical errors. Therefore, in order to keep your spoken English as grammatically correct as possible, be sure to pronounce every final *s* sound. This may be difficult in the beginning, but the more you practice, the easier it will be.

Making the Correct Sound

We write the final *s* in several ways: -*s* (stereotype*s*, she suggest*s*), -*es* (churche*s*, he misse*s* you), '*s* (the student'*s* problem), *s*' (the Americans' attitude), and we pronounce it in several different ways.

The way the final sound *s* is pronounced depends on whether it follows a voiced or voiceless sound. To determine whether a sound is voiced, put your hand on your throat as you say it. If you feel vibration, the sound is voiced; if not, it is voiceless. All vowel sounds are voiced. Following is a list of voiceless and voiced consonants; for those consonants that fall into pairs, the voiceless and voiced equivalents are shown opposite each other.

VOICELESS		VOICED	
/p/	shop, wipe	/b/	grab, robe
/t/	adapt, result	/d/	word, precede
/k/	brick, make, talk	/g/	beg, plague
/f/	chafe, graph, puff	/v/	save, improve
/th/	bath, month	/th/	bathe, breathe
/s/	grass, purse, fix	/z/	buzz, surprise
/sh/	blush, marsh	/zh/	garage, mirage
/ch/	catch, bunch	/j/	pledge, village
		/l/	hall, smile
		/r/	bore, gesture
		/m/	home, film, bomb
		/n/	align, interruption
		/ng/	bang, sampling

(*Note:* The consonants /h/, /hw/, /w/, and /y/ have not been included in the list because they are not pronounced as consonants at the end of a word.)

When a final *s* follows a voiceless sound (except /s/, /sh/, and /ch/), it has a voiceless sound. Practice saying each example word in the voiceless column, except those in the box; after you have said the word, say it again, adding a final *s*.

When a final *s* follows a voiced sound (except /z/, /zh/, and /j/), it has the voiced sound /z/. Practice saying each example word in the voiced column, except those in the box; after you have said the word, say it again, adding a final /z/. Then follow the same procedure with the following words, which end with vowel sounds:

day	key	lie	plough	chew
see	apply	borrow	draw	argue

When the final *s* comes after /s/, /z/, /sh/, /zh/, /ch/, or /j/, it is pronounced as a separate syllable, that is, as /iz/. Practice saying each word in the box; after you have said the word, say it again, adding a final /iz/.

There are three common mistakes that people make when pronouncing the final *s* sound. When you practice pronouncing the *s* sounds, keep these problems in mind and try to avoid them.

- Pronouncing the final *s* as a separate syllable at inappropriate times.

  EXAMPLE: cloth-<u>es</u>   instead of   clothes
              breath-<u>es</u>   instead of   breathes

- Pronouncing the *s* as a voiceless sound after a voiced consonant such as *l* or *r* or after a vowel.

  EXAMPLE: worker<u>s</u>   instead of   worker<u>z</u>
              Barbara'<u>s</u>   instead of   Barbara'<u>z</u>

- Omitting the sound completely.

  EXAMPLE: he go   instead of   he go<u>es</u>
              many book   instead of   many book<u>s</u>

Activity 2:   *Pronouncing the Final* S

Look at the following short conversations. Notice that the first speaker's sentences are almost the same except for the final *s* sound. Notice also that pronouncing or not pronouncing these final *s* sounds can affect the meaning of the sentence. One of your classmates will say one of the first speaker's sentences; then, depending on which sentence you hear, you will give the response that goes with that sentence.

a. FIRST SPEAKER: The American likes to be friendly to a lot of people.

   SECOND SPEAKER: Yeah, he's a friendly guy.

   FIRST SPEAKER: The Americans like to be friendly to a lot of people.

   SECOND SPEAKER: Well, maybe they're just trying to be polite.

b. FATHER: I bought the tickets for Hawaii.

   DAUGHTER: Great! When are we going?

FATHER:	I bought the ticket for Hawaii.
DAUGHTER:	What?! You're not taking me?!?

c. FIRST SPEAKER:	The Brazilian's music has a good rhythm.
SECOND SPEAKER:	Well, she's a good composer.

FIRST SPEAKER:	The Brazilian music has a good rhythm.
SECOND SPEAKER:	Yeah, it's good for dancing.

Activity 3: Practicing Emphasis, Pauses, and Final S

Read aloud one of the idiom descriptions beginning on page 227. Pay attention to the final *s* sounds as well as to your emphasis and pauses.

FINAL *ED* OF VERBS

Another problem area of pronunciation for non-native speakers of English is the final *ed* of verbs, such as the past participle form and the past tense form of regular verbs. Whether or not a listener can hear the *ed* at the end of the verb can make a difference in the way he or she interprets your sentence.

> EXAMPLES: They *plan* to go home for a vacation. (This sentence indicates that they are now planning to go.)
>
> They *planned* to go home for a vacation. (This sentence indicates that they made the plan in the past.)

Making the Correct Sound

Although the *ed* ending is always written the same way, we pronounce it in three different ways.

Just like final *s,* when *ed* follows a voiceless sound (except /t/), it too becomes voiceless and is pronounced /t/. Say each of the following verbs twice, first as written, then with the /t/ ending (for example, laugh, laughed).

laugh	help	cash
work	dress	impoverish
ask	notice	reach

When *ed* follows a voiced sound (except /d/), it is voiced and pronounced /d/. Say these verbs twice, first as written, then with the /d/ ending.

absorb	plan	care
forge	live	recoil
drag	bang	play
cram	learn	cry

When *ed* follows a final /t/ or /d/, it is pronounced as a separate syllable, that is, as /id/. Say the following verbs twice, first as written, then with the /id/ ending.

covet	head
halt	need
count	decide
wait	crowd

Activity 4: Practicing the Final ed Sound

Prepare a brief story of a recent experience you had in which you forgot to do something important. Then tell your story, paying special attention to the final *ed* sounds of verbs.

USING THE DICTIONARY—WORD STRESS

A student kept referring to "adolescents" in her speech, but she mispronounced the word. The audience, instead of listening to her points, spent all of their time trying to figure out what she was talking about. It is especially important, therefore, that you pronounce the key words of your speeches correctly. How do you find the correct pronunciation? Besides asking a native speaker of English, one of the best ways to find the correct pronunciation of a word is to look in a dictionary. In fact, when native speakers of English themselves have a question about the pronunciation of a word, they will often check their dictionary.

Different dictionaries have different ways of showing the pronunciation of words, so you should become familiar with the particular method your dic-

Figure A.1

Where to Find Pronunciation

Reprinted with permission, from *Webster's New World Dictionary, Third College Edition.* Copyright © 1988 by Simon & Schuster, Inc.

pred•e|ces•sor (pred′ə ses′ər, pred′ə ses′ər; *also* prē′də ses′-) *n.* ⟦ME *predecessour* < MFr *predecesseur* < LL *praedecessor* < L *prae-*, before (see PRE-) + *decessor*, retiring officer < *decessus*, pp. of *decedere*, to go away, depart < *de-*, from + *cedere*, to go: see CEDE⟧ **1** a person who precedes or preceded another, as in office   **2** a thing replaced by another thing, as in use   **3** an ancestor; forefather

Figure A.2

Pronunciation Guide

Reprinted with permission, from *Webster's New World Dictionary, Third College Edition.* Copyright © 1988 by Simon & Schuster, Inc.

at, āte, cär; ten, ēve; is, īce; gō, hôrn, look, to͞ol; oil, out; up, fur; ə *for unstressed vowels, as* a *in* ago, u *in* focus; ′ *as in* Latin (lat′'n); chin; she; zh *as in* azure (azh′ər); thin, *the;* ŋ *as in* ring (riŋ) *In etymologies:* * = unattested; < = derived from; > = from which; ☆ = Americanism

See inside front and back covers

tionary uses. Most dictionaries have a pronunciation key in several places. First, the pronunciation of individual words appears in parentheses after each entry (see Figure A.1). Second, at the bottom of every other page, there is often a short guide to the phonetic symbols that the dictionary uses (see Figure A.2). Third, there is often a pronunciation key inside the front cover.

Activity 5:   Reviewing Your Dictionary's Pronunciation Guide

Look at your dictionary and find the guides to pronunciation. Review the information on pronunciation that your dictionary provides.

Figure A.3

Stress Marks

↓

tol·er·ance (tăl′ər əns) *n.* 〖ME *tolleraunce* < MFr *tolerance* < L *tolerantia*〗 **1** *a)* a tolerating or being tolerant, esp. of views, beliefs, practices, etc. of other that differ from one's own *b)* freedom from bigotry or prejudice **2** the amount of variation allowed from a standard, accuracy, etc.; specif., *a)* the amount that coins are legally allowed to vary from a standard of weight, fineness, etc. *b)* the difference between the allowable maximum and minimum sizes of some mechanical part, as a basis for determining the accuracy of a fitting **3** the ability to endure **4** *Med.* the natural or developed ability to resist the effects of the continued or increasing use of a drug, etc.

Notice in Figure A.1 that the dictionary divides the word *predecessor* into parts and separates each part with a dot or a line—*pred·e|ces·sor.* You should pronounce each syllable as a separate unit. In English, however, some syllables are pronounced louder, longer, and at a higher pitch than other syllables. How do you know which syllable to pronounce in this way? The dictionary uses a stress mark (′) to show you. Look at the dictionary entry for the word *tolerance.* Notice that the stress mark follows the first syllable (see Figure A.3). This means that you should pronounce the word like this: *TOLerance.* Make sure that the first syllable is louder and longer and has higher pitch than the others. Please note that British and some other dictionaries may use a different system for marking stress, so it is important for you to become familiar with the system that is used in your dictionary.

You need to stress the correct syllable not only because this will result in proper pronunciation, but also because you can sometimes change the meaning of words depending upon which syllable you stress. For example, look at the following words:

ex′port: (noun) an object sent to another country

ex·port′: (verb) to send something to another country

con′vict: (noun) a person guilty of a crime

con·vict′: (verb) to prove somebody guilty of a crime

Therefore, if you are not sure about the correct stress of a word, be sure to look it up in your dictionary.

Figure A.4

Multiple Stress Marks

Reprinted with permission, from *Webster's New World Dictionary, Third College Edition*. Copyright © 1988 by Simon & Schuster, Inc.

as·sim|i·late (ə sim′ə lāt′) *vt.* -lat′|ed, -lat′ing ⟦ME *assimilaten* < L *assimilatus*, pp. of *assimilare* < ad-, to + *similare*, make similar < *similis*, like: see SAME⟧ **1** to change (food) into a form that can be taken up by, and made part of, the body tissues; absorb into the body **2** to absorb and incorporate into one's thinking **3** to absorb (groups of different cultures) into the main cultural body **4** to make like or alike; cause to resemble; with *to* **5** [Now Rare] to compare or liken **6** *Linguis.* to cause to undergo assimilation —*vi.* **1** to become like or alike **2** to be absorbed and incorporated **3** *Linguis.* to undergo assimilation —as·sim′|i·la|ble (-ə lə bəl) *adj.*

Activity 6: *Practicing Word Stresses*

Practice saying the following words. Make sure to pronounce the stress correctly.

cul′tu·ral   pro′ject

lit′er·a·cy   pro·ject′

ne′ces·sa·ry   • ex·pres′sion

Sometimes two syllables in a word are stressed, as in the dictionary entry for *assimilate*. When more than one syllable is stressed, one syllable receives more emphasis than the other. This dictionary shows this by using a heavy stress mark for the stronger syllable and a lighter stress mark for the other stressed syllable (see Figure A.4).

Activity 7: *Practicing Words with More Than One Stress*

Practice saying the following words. Make sure that you pronounce the stress correctly.

con·fed′er·a′tion   nat′u·ral·i·za′tion

e·lim′i·nate′   re·sus′ci·ta′tion

na′tiv·iz′m   ho′mo·ge·ne′i·ty

per′i·od′i·cal   dis·crim′i·na′tion

Activity 8:   Practicing Word Stresses and Syllabication

Following are some sentences from the English-only article in Unit 6. Look up the underlined words in your dictionary. Divide them into syllables and put stress marks after the stressed syllables. Practice saying each sentence; pay attention to your word stress.

a. We believe that such laws are contrary to the spirit of <u>tolerance</u> and <u>diversity</u> <u>embodied</u> in our Constitution.

b. Some states <u>restrict</u> bilingual education programs, <u>prohibit</u> multi-lingual <u>ballots,</u> or <u>forbid</u> non-English government services in general.

c. In some states, the laws were passed <u>decades</u> ago during <u>upsurges</u> of <u>nativism,</u> but most were passed within the last few years.

WORD STRESS PATTERNS

Knowing which syllable to stress when pronouncing English words can sometimes be difficult, especially when suffixes (endings) are added to the words. When the following suffixes are added, words tend to keep their original stress patterns:

moun′tain	moun′tain•<u>ous</u>	friend′ly	friend′li•<u>ness</u>
com′fort	com′fort•a•<u>ble</u>	plen′ty	plen′ti•<u>ful</u>
vis′it	vis′i•<u>tor</u>	for′tune	for′tu•<u>nate</u>

However, when the suffixes *tion, ity,* and *ic* are added, the stress always falls on the syllable immediately preceding the suffix.

-tion

Your instructor will first pronounce the words in column A and then those in column B. Listen carefully and place a stress mark (′) after the stressed syllable in each word.

COLUMN A (VERBS)	COLUMN B (NOUNS)
com mu ni cate	com mu ni ca tion
con trib ute	con tri bu tion
il lus trate	il lus tra tion
in tro duce	in tro duc tion
par tic i pate	par tic i pa tion
in ter rupt	in ter rup tion
in form	in for ma tion

1. Notice that the position of stressed syllables in the words in column A can change from word to word. Notice, however, that the stressed syllables in column B are always in the same position. What is the stress pattern associated with words that end in *-tion*? Practice saying the words in column B. Pay attention to your word stress.

2. Notice how the position of the stressed syllable can change from the verb form to the noun form of the word. Notice also how some of the vowel sounds change when they are not stressed. For example, when you say *contribute*, the *i* is a stressed vowel, and you pronounce it like the vowel in the word *bit*. However, when you say *contribution*, this syllable is now not stressed, and you pronounce the *i* like the vowel in the word *bus*. Vowel sounds in English often change when they are unstressed. Now listen to your teacher pronounce the pairs of words. Can you hear which vowel sounds change? Practice saying the pairs of words yourself. Pay attention to your word stress and vowel sounds.

3. Mark the stressed syllables in the following words. Then practice saying these words. Pay attention to your word stress.

im mi gra tion	ed u ca tion
rec og ni tion	pre con cep tion
gen er a tion	

4. Mark the stressed syllables in the underlined words. Then practice saying the following sentences:

   a. When you're in an informal <u>conversation</u>, you can get someone's <u>attention</u> by saying, "Well" or "You know."

   b. If you can't follow someone's ideas, you can ask for <u>repetition</u>.

-ity

Your instructor will first pronounce the words in column A and then those in column B. Listen carefully, and place a stress mark after the stressed syllable in each word.

COLUMN A (ADJECTIVES)	COLUMN B (NOUNS)
for mal	for mal i ty
ob jec tive	ob jec tiv i ty
am big u ous	am bi gu i ty
com plex	com plex i ty
ac tive	ac tiv i ty
fa mil iar	fa mil i ar i ty

1. Notice that all of the words in column B end with *-ity*. What is the stress pattern associated with the words that end in *-ity*? Practice saying the words in column B yourself. Pay attention to your word stress.

2. Listen to your teacher pronounce the pairs of words. Can you hear the vowel sounds change from the adjective form to the noun form of the words? Practice saying the pairs of words yourself. Pay attention to your word stress and vowel sounds.

3. Mark the stressed syllables in the following words. Practice saying these words. Pay attention to your word stress.

le gal i ty	in fin i ty
sim plic i ty	mo bil i ty
se lec tiv i ty	

4. Mark the stressed syllables in the underlined words. Then practice saying the following sentences:

   a. A few people have the <u>ability</u> to speak with <u>authority</u> in front of a group of people.

   b. A speaker needs to consider the <u>suitability</u> of his topic.

   c. A speaker also needs to have a certain amount of <u>sensitivity</u> toward his audience.

-ic

Your instructor will first pronounce the words in column A and then those in column B. Listen carefully and place a stress mark after the stressed syllable in each word.

COLUMN A (NOUNS)	COLUMN B (ADJECTIVES)
pe ri od	pe ri od ic
strat e gy	stra te gic
trau ma	trau mat ic
id i om	id i o mat ic
pho to graph	pho to graph ic
sym pho ny	sym phon ic

1. Notice that all of the words in column B end with *-ic*. What is the stress pattern associated with words that end in *-ic*?

2. Listen to your teacher pronounce the pairs of words. Can you hear the vowel sounds change from the noun form to the adjective form of the words? Practice saying the pairs of words yourself. Pay attention to your word stress and vowel sounds.

3. Mark the stressed syllables in the underlined words. Then practice saying the following sentences.

   a. Being nervous is <u>characteristic</u> of most speakers.

   b. Most audiences feel <u>sympathetic</u> toward speakers.

   c. Audiences enjoy speakers who are <u>enthusiastic</u> about their topics.

4. Notice that this same stress pattern generally holds true for the suffixes *ical* and *ically* (for example, the′ater, thea′trical, thea′trically).

USING THE DICTIONARY—VOWEL SOUNDS

You have seen that your dictionary can help you to pronounce words correctly. If you were to look up the word *embargo,* you might see em•bar•go (im bär′gō). You know from the previous section about word stress that the dot symbol (•) divides the word into three syllables and that the stress marks (′) tell you which syllables to stress. But what does the symbol over the letter *o* (ō) mean?

Because most people don't know what these symbols mean, especially the vowels, the dictionary provides a guide to the pronunciation symbols it uses. At the bottom of the same page on which you find *embargo* is the following pronunciation guide to vowels:*

at, āte, cär; ten, ēve; is, īce; gō, hôrn, look, tōol; oil, out; up, fᵤr;
ə *for unstressed vowels, as* a *in* ago, u *in* focus;

Each symbol is contained in a short, common word that contains that sound. You know, therefore, that you should pronounce ā like the vowel sound in *ate,* that you should pronounce ōo like the vowel sound in *tool,* and that you should pronounce ə like the first vowel sound in *ago.*

Different dictionaries may use different symbols, so be sure to become familiar with the symbols that your dictionary uses. Every dictionary, however, provides you with some kind of guide. If you are not sure how to pronounce the words that the dictionary uses in the pronunciation guide, be sure to ask a native speaker to pronounce them for you.

Activity 9:   Using Pronunciation Guides

Below are some words and their pronunciations. Practice using the pronunciation guide to help you pronounce these words correctly.

vary (var′i)	image (im′ij)
conceal (kən•sēl′)	insecure (in•si•kyoor′)
stern (stᵤrn)	grate (grāt)
feasible (fē′zə•bl)	dread (dred)
hero (hēr′ō)	astonish (ə•stän′ish)
quest (kwest)	preface (pref′is)
object (əb•jekt′)	excerpt (ek′sᵤrpt)
delight (di•līt′)	

---

* *Webster's New World Dictionary, Third College Edition* (New York: Simon & Schuster, 1988).

Activity 10:   Using Your Dictionary

Following are some sentences from the excerpts on the homeless in Unit 4. Look up the underlined words in your dictionary. Make sure that you know how to pronounce them. Try to pronounce the stress as well as the sounds correctly. Practice saying the complete sentences. Pay attention to pauses and emphasis.

a. The growing <u>phenomenon</u> of homelessness is nothing short of a national <u>disgrace</u>.

b. Meanwhile, <u>advocates</u> for the homeless—and their <u>allies</u> in Congress—are <u>gearing</u> up for a major <u>campaign</u> to force the Bush administration to do more.

c. A class war is <u>brewing</u> between angry <u>indigents</u> and <u>disgruntled</u> citizens forced to step out of their way.

d. Part of the reason for the growing <u>backlash</u> is simply <u>sheer</u> numbers.

e. Public <u>disfavor</u> may also be <u>spurred</u> by changes in the makeup of the homeless population.

Index